MICROBIOLOGY PRACTICAL HAND BOOK (FOR MEDICAL SCIENCE STUDENTS)

DR. DINESH C. SHARMA | DR. SWEETY AHLAWAT

Made with ♥ on the Notion Press Platform
www.notionpress.com

The First Edition of this Book Entitled "Microbiology Practical Hand Book (For Medical Sciences Students)" is solely dedicated to the almighty GOD.

Contents

Foreword

The purpose of Microbiology Practical Handbook (For Medical Sciences Students), is to address and resolve common challenges encountered during microbiology practicals.

In the ever-evolving field of medical sciences, a strong foundation in microbiology is indispensable. Practical experience in microbiology not only solidifies theoretical knowledge but also equips students with the essential skills required for a career in healthcare and research. However, navigating the complexities of microbiology practicals can often present challenges that hinder the learning process.

Microbiology Practical Handbook (For Medical Sciences Students) is crafted to bridge this gap. This handbook emerges from a deep understanding of the common hurdles faced by students and aims to provide practical solutions and clear guidance. It is designed to be an accessible and comprehensive resource, offering step-by-step instructions, troubleshooting tips, and insights into best practices for laboratory work.

Authored with the needs of medical sciences students in mind, this handbook serves as both a reference and a companion throughout the practical aspects of microbiology education. It empowers students to approach their laboratory sessions with confidence, clarity, and competence.

I am confident that this handbook will become an invaluable tool in your academic journey, enhancing your practical skills and deepening your understanding of microbiological techniques. May it inspire curiosity, foster a passion for discovery, and contribute to your success in the fascinating world of microbiology

Preface

Microbiology Practical Handbook (For Medical Sciences Students) is designed to bridge the gap between classroom theory and practical application. This handbook aims to provide a comprehensive, user-friendly guide to the laboratory techniques and procedures that are fundamental to microbiology. It addresses common challenges and pitfalls, offering clear instructions and practical solutions to help students gain confidence and competence in their laboratory work.

Each chapter is thoughtfully organized to cover key practical aspects, including preparation, execution, and analysis of microbiological experiments. We have included detailed protocols, troubleshooting tips, and best practices to ensure that students can approach their practicals with clarity and precision. Additionally, the book incorporates real-world examples and scenarios to enhance understanding and application of microbiological principles.

Our goal with this handbook is to support students in developing a robust skill set and to foster a deeper appreciation for the field of microbiology. We believe that mastering these practical skills will not only contribute to academic success but also lay a strong foundation for future professional endeavors.

We hope that this handbook serves as a valuable resource throughout your studies, helping to illuminate the complexities of microbiology and to inspire a lifelong curiosity about the microscopic world. May it guide you in your practical endeavors and support you in achieving your academic and professional goals.

Welcome to an exciting journey through the practical aspects of microbiology.

Acknowledgements

The creation of Microbiology Practical Handbook (For Medical Sciences Students) has been a collaborative and rewarding journey..

First and foremost, I would like to extend my heartfelt thanks to the almighty authority, my colleagues and mentors. Their guidance, expertise, and encouragement have been invaluable throughout the development of this book.

I am also deeply grateful to my students, whose questions, feedback, and experiences have highlighted the common challenges faced during microbiology practicals. Their input has been crucial in identifying the practical needs that this handbook aims to address.

A sincere thank you goes to the academic and administrative staff at Sanskriti University, Mathura for their unwavering support and resources, which have facilitated the creation of this book. Their commitment to excellence in education and research has been a constant source of inspiration.

To my family and friends, thank you for your patience, encouragement, and understanding during the countless hours dedicated to writing and revising this handbook. Your support has been a pillar of strength throughout this endeavor.

This handbook is the result of collective effort and collaboration. It is my hope that it serves as a valuable resource for students and educators alike, helping to make the study of microbiology both accessible and enriching.

Thank you all for your contributions and support.

Prologue

Microbiology is often described as the study of the invisible world. Through microscopes and laboratory techniques, we unveil the intricate and dynamic interactions of microorganisms that profoundly affect our lives, health, and environment. For students in medical sciences, the journey from theoretical concepts to practical expertise is both exhilarating and demanding.

The practical laboratory work in microbiology is more than just an academic exercise; it is a gateway to understanding how microbial processes influence human health and disease. Yet, for many students, this journey can be fraught with challenges. From mastering aseptic techniques to interpreting complex experimental results, the path to proficiency is not always straightforward.

Microbiology Practical Handbook (For Medical Sciences Students) has been created to guide you through this intricate landscape. This book serves as a comprehensive companion, meticulously designed to address the common hurdles and uncertainties that arise during microbiology practicals. It is built on the premise that practical knowledge is crucial to solidifying theoretical understanding and that clear, actionable guidance can make the difference between confusion and clarity.

In these pages, you will find detailed protocols, practical tips, and troubleshooting advice that aim to demystify the laboratory processes and make them more accessible. Each section is crafted to provide step-by-step instructions and to offer insight into the rationale behind each procedure. By presenting practical skills in a structured and relatable manner, we hope to build your confidence and competence in the laboratory setting.

This handbook is not just a collection of methods but a reflection of the passion for microbiology that drives both educators and students alike. It embodies the commitment to fostering a deeper understanding of the microbial world and to equipping future medical professionals with the tools they need to excel.

As you embark on your journey through the practical aspects of microbiology, may this handbook serve as both a resource and a source of inspiration. It is our hope that it will facilitate your learning, enhance your laboratory skills, and ignite a lifelong curiosity about the microscopic universe that surrounds us.

Welcome to the world of microbiology, where every experiment is an opportunity to discover and learn.

CHAPTER ONE

Objective no – 01: To demonstrate the Microbiology Lab Practices and Safety Rules

- Wash your hands with disinfectants when you arrive at the lab and again before you leave.
- Wear laboratory coats in the lab. Students with long hair must put up the hair.
- At the start and end of each laboratory session, students should clean their assigned bench-top area with a disinfectant solution provided. That space should then be kept neat, clean, and uncluttered throughout each laboratory period.
- Eating or drinking in the laboratory is not permitted. No mouth pipetting.
- Label everything clearly. Sterilize equipment and materials.
- Avoid loose fitting items of clothing. Wear appropriate shoes in the laboratory.
- Report any breakage of equipment to the instructor.
- Report any personal accidents such as cuts to the instructor at once.
- Turn off Bunsen burner when not in use.
- Discard all cultures and used glassware into the container labeled CONTAMINATED. (This container will later be sterilized.) Plastic or other disposable items should be discarded separately from glassware in containers to be sterilized.
- Never place contaminated pipettes on the bench top.
- When you flame sterilize with alcohol, be sure that you do not have any papers under you.
- Before beginning your laboratory exercise, wash off the bench top with the disinfectant provided. When exercises are completed, wash off the bench top again. Always wash your hands with soap and water before leaving the laboratory.
- Before leaving the laboratory, see that all the equipments are in the proper location and gas and water turned off.
- Purchase a fine point, waterproof marker and small roll of masking tape. Use them to clearly label your cultures.
- If you should spill or drop a culture or if any type of accident occurs, call the instructor immediately. Place a paper towel over any spill and pour disinfectant over the towel. Let the disinfectant stand for 15 minutes and then clean the spill with fresh paper towels. Remember to discard the paper towels in the proper receptacle and wash your hands carefully.
- Disinfect work areas before and after use with 70% alcohol or fresh 10% bleach. Laboratory equipment and work surfaces should be decontaminated with an appropriate disinfectant on a routine basis and especially after spills, splashes or other contamination.
- Replace caps on reagents, solution bottles and bacterial cultures. Do not open petri dishes in the lab unless absolutely necessary.
- Cultures are not to be removed from the laboratory unless the instructor gives permission.
- Always place culture tubes (broth and slants) in the upright position in a rack or basket for incubation or disposal.

- Dispose off all solid waste materials in a biohazard bag and autoclave it before discarding in the regular trash.
- Treat all cultures as potentially pathogenic, *i.e.*, flood areas with disinfectant if cultures are spilled, wash hands after contact and notify your instructor at once.
- Read the instructions carefully before beginning an exercise. Also, make sure you have all the materials needed for the exercise at hand before you commence the experiment. Ask the instructor for clarification of any points about which you are in doubt.
- Flame the inoculating loop or needle immediately before and after use. If viscous material is present on the loop or needle, dry it at the side of the flame before placing it directly in the flame.
- Laboratory note books must be kept up-to-date. Illustrations should be done when requested.
- Make sure you consult the instructor to dispose of the cultures that are not needed any longer. Remove all labels and markings from the tubes before disposing of them; do not discard anything into the sinks.
- Please inform your instructor if you have any medical condition that could potentially affect your safety in the laboratory (eg: diabetes, epilepsy, immunosuppression etc.). This information will help the instructor to deal with any emergency that would arise. The information will be treated confidentially and it will not affect their ability to participate in the laboratory activities.
- Be systematic and logical. Keep a faithful record of all the experiments and observations. Update it regularly and submit it for evaluation at the end of each exercise.
- Work either using laminar air flow chamber or light the burner at least five minutes prior to making any inoculations and work near the burner.

Objective no – 02: Basic Requirements of Microbiology Laboratory

Microbiology Lab Practices and Safety Rules

- Wash your hands with disinfectants when you arrive at the lab and again before you leave.
- Wear laboratory coats in the lab. Students with long hair must put up the hair.
- At the start and end of each laboratory session, students should clean their assigned bench-top area with a disinfectant solution provided. That space should then be kept neat, clean, and uncluttered throughout each laboratory period.
- Eating or drinking in the laboratory is not permitted. No mouth pipetting.
- Label everything clearly. Sterilize equipment and materials.
- Avoid loose fitting items of clothing. Wear appropriate shoes in the laboratory.
- Report any breakage of equipment to the instructor.
- Report any personal accidents such as cuts to the instructor at once.
- Turn off Bunsen burner when not in use.
- Discard all cultures and used glassware into the container labeled CONTAMINATED. (This container will later be sterilized.) Plastic or other disposable items should be discarded separately from glassware in containers to be sterilized.
- Never place contaminated pipettes on the bench top.
- When you flame sterilize with alcohol, be sure that you do not have any papers under you.
- Before beginning your laboratory exercise, wash off the bench top with the disinfectant provided. When exercises are completed, wash off the bench top again. Always wash your hands with soap and water before leaving the laboratory.
- Before leaving the laboratory, see that all the equipments are in the proper location and gas and water turned off.
- Purchase a fine point, waterproof marker and small roll of masking tape. Use them to clearly label your cultures.
- If you should spill or drop a culture or if any type of accident occurs, call the instructor immediately. Place a paper towel over any spill and pour disinfectant over the towel. Let the disinfectant stand for 15 minutes and then clean the spill with fresh paper towels. Remember to discard the paper towels in the proper receptacle and wash your hands carefully.
- Disinfect work areas before and after use with 70% alcohol or fresh 10% bleach. Laboratory equipment and work surfaces should be decontaminated with an appropriate disinfectant on a routine basis and especially after spills, splashes or other contamination.
- Replace caps on reagents, solution bottles and bacterial cultures. Do not open petri dishes in the lab unless absolutely necessary.
- Cultures are not to be removed from the laboratory unless the instructor gives permission.
- Always place culture tubes (broth and slants) in the upright position in a rack or basket for incubation or disposal.
- Dispose off all solid waste materials in a biohazard bag and autoclave it before discarding in the regular trash.

- Treat all cultures as potentially pathogenic, i.e., flood areas with disinfectant if cultures are spilled, wash hands after contact and notify your instructor at once.
- Read the instructions carefully before beginning an exercise. Also, make sure you have all the materials needed for the exercise at hand before you commence the experiment. Ask the instructor for clarification of any points about which you are in doubt.
- Flame the inoculating loop or needle immediately before and after use. If viscous material is present on the loop or needle, dry it at the side of the flame before placing it directly in the flame.
- Laboratory note books must be kept up-to-date. Illustrations should be done when requested.
- Make sure you consult the instructor to dispose of the cultures that are not needed any longer. Remove all labels and markings from the tubes before disposing of them; do not discard anything into the sinks.
- Please inform your instructor if you have any medical condition that could potentially affect your safety in the laboratory (eg: diabetes, epilepsy, immunosuppression etc.). This information will help the instructor to deal with any emergency that would arise. The information will be treated confidentially and it will not affect their ability to participate in the laboratory activities.
- Be systematic and logical. Keep a faithful record of all the experiments and observations. Update it regularly and submit it for evaluation at the end of each exercise.
- Work either using laminar air flow chamber or light the burner at least five minutes prior to making any inoculations and work near the burner.

CHAPTER THREE

Objective no – 03: To Study the colony characteristics of bacteria

Principle:

When grown on a variety of media, microorganisms will exhibit the difference in the microscopic appearance of their broth. These differences are called cultural characteristics and are used as a basis for separating microorganism into taxonomic groups. The cultural characteristics for all taxon microorganisms are contained in Bergey's Manual of systematic bacteriology.

Growth on Solid Media

The following characters of colony are noted:

1. Size: inmillimeter
2. Shape: circular /irregular
3. Surface : smooth, rough,granular
4. Elevation : flat, low convex, high convex, raised, umbonate,umbulate
5. Edge: entire, undulate, lobate, crenated, fimbricate,ciliate
6. Opacity : opaque, translucent,transparent
7. Colour ofcolony
8. Consistency : mucoid,friable
9. Other properties : hemolysis, pigmentation, swarming

Morphology on nutrient agar slants:

The isolated bacteria can be identified based on their colony characteristics in the following manner-

1. Degree of growth : scanty, moderate,abundant
2. Surface : smooth, rough, granular
3. Elevation : convex, flat,raised
4. Edge : entire, undulate, crenate
5. Opacity : opaque, translucent,transparent
6. Consistency : firm, butyrosis, powdery, mucoid, membranous
7. Colour of Colony : creamy white, lemon yellow, bluish green
8. Form : filiform, echinulated, beaded, effuse, rhizoid
9. Changes in Medium : changes in colour, pitting ofagar

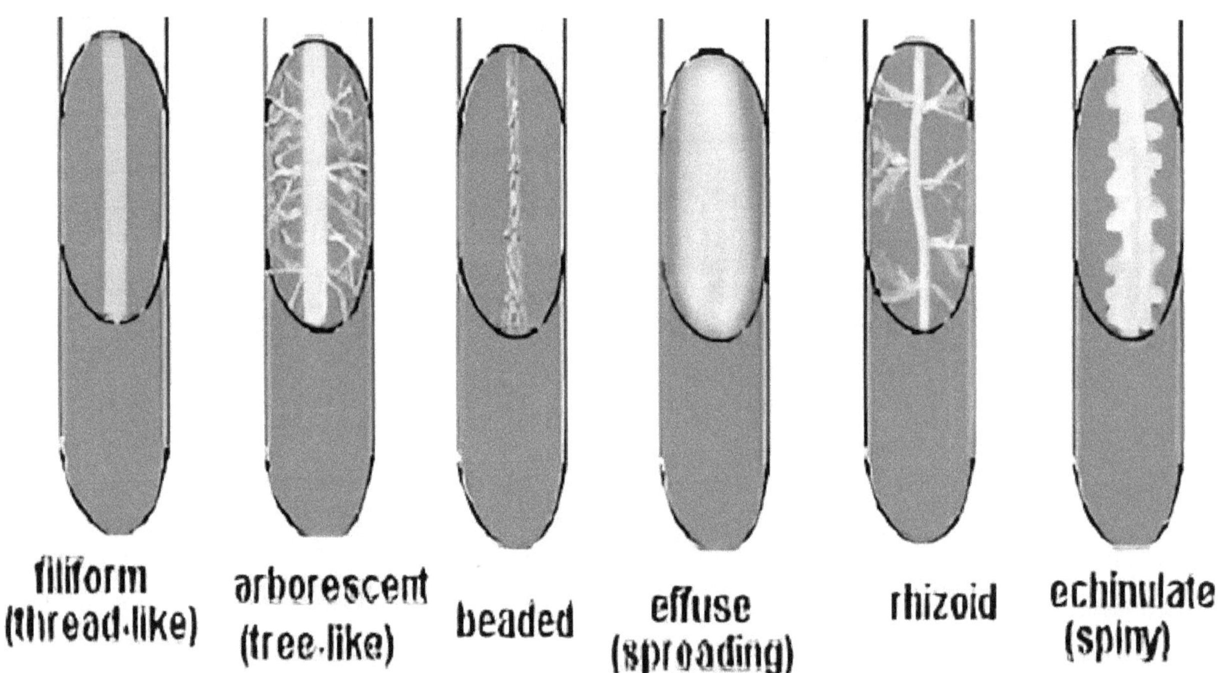

Different types of Growth on Slant

Growth in Liquid Media-

The liquid medium (nutrient broth, peptone water and other liquid media) the following characteristics are noted:

The degree of growth : scanty, moderate, abundant presence of turbidity and its nature (uniformturbidity) presence of deposits, pellicle formation on surface & itsquality.

Morphology on Nutrient Agar Plates

These demonstrate well isolated colonies and are evaluated in the following manner-

1. *Size*: pinpoint, moderate, small orlarge
2. *Colour of thecolony*

    a. Form : the shape of the colony:
    b. Circular : unbroken, peripheraledge
    c. Irregular : intended, peripheraledge
    d. Rhizoid : root like, spreadinggrowth

3. *Margin*: The appearance of the outer edge of the colony is described asfollows

    a. Entire : sharp
    b. Lobate : markedindentations
    c. Undulate : wavyindentations
    d. Serrate : tooth likeappearance
    e. Filamentous: thread like, spreadingedge

4. *Elevation* : the degree to which the colony growth is raised on the surface is described asfollows:

    a. Flat : elevation notdiscernible

b. Raised : slightlyelevated
c. Convex : dome shaped elevation
d. Umbonate : raised with elevated convex central region

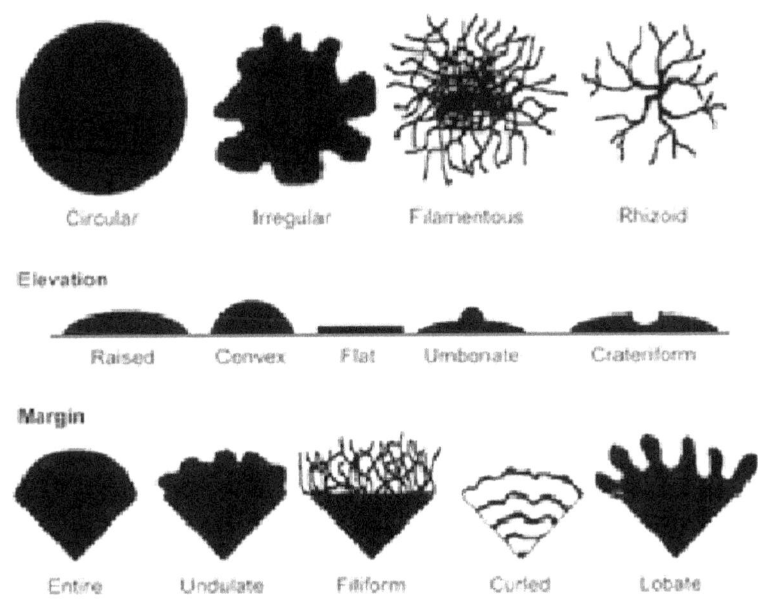

Culture Characterstics on Media

CHAPTER FOUR

Objective no – 04: Preparation of Culture media for bacteria

The culture media is a composition of various essential and non-essential nutrients which are required for the growth of microorganisms such as bacteria as well as fungus. Culture media can be divided in various categories such as liquid media (broth- without Agar), solid media (Agar media- with Agar), Agar, a polysaccharide, is used in the media as a solidifying agent. Agar can be liquefied at 60 to 75°C and remains solidified at or below 50°C.

Requirements:

Peptone, beef extract, NaCl, agar powder, distilled water, autoclave, conical flask, laminar air flow, test tubes, Bunsen burner etc

A. Nutrient broth

Peptone 5.0 gms

Beef extract 3.0 gms

NaCl 5.0 gms

Distilled water 1000 ml

B. NutrientAagar

Beef Extract 3.0 gms

Peptone 5.0 gms

Agar 20.0 gms

NaCl 5.0 gms

Distilled water 1000 ml

NOTE* All the ingredients are dissolved in warm water and the pH is adjusted to 7.2-7.6. Autoclaved at 121°C, 15 lbs for 15 minutes.

Procedure:

1. Weigh the constituents on a digital weighing balance.
2. Add the contents to 800 ml of distilled water.
3. Heat to mix the contents and make the final volume to1000ml.
4. Adjust the pH to7.0 ± 0.1

Results:

Nutrient broth: Liquid medium

Nutrient agar: Solid medium

Error analysis:

Constituents should be weighed accurately. pH should be measured before autoclaving otherwise growth maybe affected.

Precautions:

Care should be taken while handling autoclave and hot culture media.

CHAPTER FIVE

Objective no – 05: Preparation of Blood Agar Media

Blood agar media is a type of enriched bacterial growth medium used in microbiology laboratories. Its major components and thier impportance are as follows:

1. **Agar**: This is a gelatinous substance derived from seaweed that solidifies the medium, providing a stable surface for bacterial growth.
2. **Blood**: Typically, sheep's blood is used in blood agar. It is added to the agar while it is still in a liquid state. The blood serves as an enriched nutrient source for bacteria, providing essential growth factors such as vitamins, amino acids, and minerals.
3. **Purpose**: Blood agar is primarily used to cultivate fastidious organisms that require specific nutrients not provided by basic media. The blood in the agar supports the growth of these organisms, allowing for their isolation and identification.
4. **Types of Hemolysis**: Blood agar can also be used to distinguish different types of hemolysis:

   ◦ **Alpha hemolysis**: Partial hemolysis of red blood cells, which results in a greenish discoloration around the bacterial colonies.
   ◦ **Beta hemolysis**: Complete hemolysis of red blood cells, leading to a clear zone surrounding bacterial colonies.
   ◦ **Gamma hemolysis**: No hemolysis occurs; there is no change in the appearance of the agar around the colonies.

5. **Applications**: It is widely used in clinical microbiology for the isolation and identification of pathogenic bacteria from clinical samples, such as blood, urine, and wound swabs. It helps in determining the hemolytic properties of bacteria, which can aid in their classification and identification.

In summary, blood agar is essential in microbiology for its ability to support the growth of a wide range of bacteria, particularly those with complex nutritional requirements, and for its diagnostic utility in identifying hemolytic characteristics of bacterial colonies.

Requirements:

Bunsen burner, autoclave, magnetic stirrer, refrigerator, Sterile Petri dishes, laminar hood, incubator, beaker, measuring cylinder, spatula, conical flask, weighing balance, Peptone, beef extract/yeast extract, agar, NaCl, Distilled water

Composition of Blood Agar:

Tryptone : 15 gm
Phytone or soytone : 5 gm
NaCl : 5 gm
Agar : 15 gm
Distilled water : 1 liter

Heat with agitation to dissolve agar. Autoclave 15 min at 121°C. Cool to 50°C. Add 5 ml defibrinated sheep red blood cells to 100 ml melted agar. Mix and pour 20 ml portions into sterile 15 × 100 mm Petri dishes. The final pH of the base is 7.3 ± 0.2.

Procedure:

- About 40 grams of the prepared medium is added to 1000 ml of distilled or deionized water.
- The suspension is heated up to boiling to dissolve the medium completely.
- It is then sterilized by autoclaving it at 15 lbs pressure and 121°C for about 15 minutes.
- The medium is then taken out of the autoclaved and cooled to about 40-45°C.
- To this, 5% v/v sterile defibrinated blood is added aseptically and mixed well.
- The media is then poured into sterile Petri plates under sterile conditions.
- Once the media solidifies, the plates can be placed in the hot air oven at a lower heat setting for a few minutes to remove any moisture present on the plates before use.

Precautions:
Proper care must be taken while handling the media during sterilization.

CHAPTER SIX

Objective no – 06: Preparation of Chocolate Agar Media

Chocolate agar, also known as heated blood agar or enriched blood agar, is a type of bacterial growth medium used for cultivating fastidious organisms, particularly those that require additional nutrients not provided by ordinary growth media like nutrient agar.

Requirements:

Bunsen burner, autoclave, magnetic stirrer, refrigerator, Sterile Petri dishes, laminar hood, incubator, beaker, measuring cylinder, glass rod, spatula, conical flask, Peptone, beef extract/yeast extract, agar, NaCl, Distilled water

Principle:

Chocolate Agar Base, with the addition of supplements, gives excellent growth of fastidious organisms without overgrowth by contaminating organisms. Casein and animal tissue digest that provides the organism with nitrogenous nutrients, amino acids, and other elements essential for the growth of the organisms. As *Neisseria* species are highly sensitive to toxic substances such as fatty acids, hence the addition of cornstarch helps neutralize possible toxic metabolites, while potassium phosphate helps maintain a uniform pH during growth. Sodium chloride maintains osmotic equilibrium thereby maintaining the integrity of cells.

Composition:

Casein/Animal Tissue Digest .... 15.0 g

Cornstarch .... 1.0 g

Potassium Phosphate, Dibasic .... 4.0 g

Potassium Phosphate, Monobasic .... 1.0 g

Sodium Chloride .... 5.0 g

Agar .... 10.0 g

Hemoglobin Solution (2%) .... 500 0 mL

Isovitox Enrichment .... 10.0 mL

pH 7.2 ± 0.2

Blood: Typically sheep blood is used. It provides essential nutrients such as vitamins, amino acids, and other growth factors necessary for the growth of certain bacteria.

Agar: A gelatinous substance derived from seaweed that solidifies the medium and provides a stable surface for bacterial growth.

Chocolate agar is called so because the heating process during preparation changes the color and consistency of the agar, making it look similar to milk chocolate.

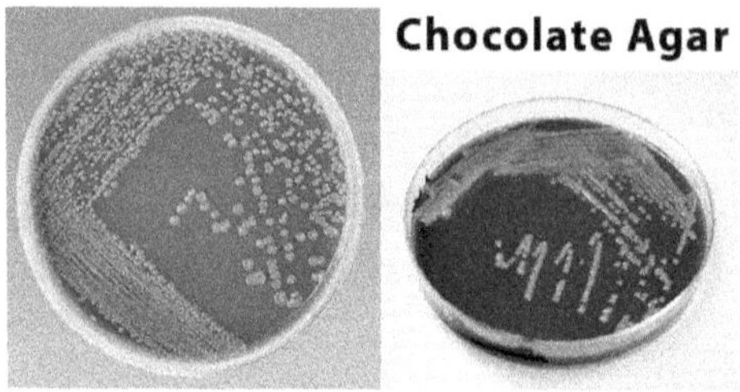

Chocolate Agar Media

Procedure:

Preparation of the hemoglobin solution

Add hemoglobin to distilled water and bring volume to 500 ml. Mix thoroughly and autoclave for 15 min at 15lbs pressure at 21°C. Cool at 45°C -50°C.

Preparation of medium

Add components except for hemoglobin solution to distilled water and bring volume to 500ml. Mix thoroughly. Gently heat until boiling. Autoclave for 15 min at 15lbs pressure at 21°C. Cool at 45°C -50°C. Add 500ml of sterile hemoglobin solution and mix thoroughly. Pour into sterile Petri dishes or distribute into sterile tubes.

Precautions:

1. Proper care must be taken while handling and distributing the media in sterile culture tubes.
2. Only clean glassware should be used for the preparation of media.

CHAPTER SEVEN

Objective no – 07: Preparation of Meat Extract Broth

Beef meet broth is a non-selective nutrient medium containing beef extract and peptone as a source of nitrogen and carbon source, long-chain amino acids, vitamins, and other essential nutrients. Sodium chloride is a source of electrolytes.

Many organisms to be studied in medical bacteriology are either pathogens or commensals of the human body, and to obtain suitable growth the artificial culture medium should provide nutrients and a pH (about 7.2) approximating those of the tissues and body fluids. For routine purposes, many of these nutrients are supplied by aqueous extracts of beef and peptone, which is a product of the digestion of protein. B.meat Broth can be used as a general-purpose nutrient medium and is also recommended for the preparation of pure culture of Candida species for carrying out fermentation studies.

Requirement:

laminar air flow, incubator, beakers, test tubes, measuring cylinder, glass rod, spatula, conical flask, Balance, cotton plugs, Peptone, beef extract/yeast extract, agar, NaCl, Distilled water

Composition (for 1000 ml):

Peptic digest of animal tissue...................... 10 gms
Beef extract...................... 3.0 gms
Sodium chloride...................... 5.0 gms
Distilled Water...................... 1000 ml
Final pH (at 25°C) 7.2 ± 0.2

Procedure:

- Dissolve 18.0 grams in 1000 ml purified/distilled water.
- Heat if necessary to dissolve the medium completely.
- Dispense in tubes or flasks or as desired.
- Sterilize by autoclaving at 15 psi pressure (121°C) for 15 minutes.

Precautions:

1. Carefully store the media below 30°C in a tightly closed container and the prepared medium at 2-8°C. Use before the expiry date on the label.

2. Weighing should be accurate and pH must be adjusted before putting for autoclave.

CHAPTER EIGHT

Objective no – 08: Inoculation of Culture on the Media

A pure culture consists of only one species of microbes. If another species of microbes is accidentally introduced in to the pure culture, then the culture is contaminated and it is called mixed culture. To get a pure culture, culturing and sub culturing of bacteria should be done in a condition or environment which is free from all types of microbes (to avoid contamination). This condition is called aseptic condition and the procedure for obtaining and maintaining pure culture in this aseptic condition is called aseptic transfer technique. Inoculation of culture in to media for the cultivation and identification of smears is both fundamental and important.

Requirement:

Laminar hood, Inoculation needle/wire loop, spirit lamp, match box, cotton, spirit/70% ethyl alcohol, glass spreader, metal forceps, glass petridish, flask, sterile test tubes, bacterial culture, Bunsen burner

Procedure:

A. BROTH CULTURE:

1. Clean with disinfectant.

2. Place the Bunsen burner in front of you, all tubes and other equipment in a suitable location which will allow you to reach them without any difficulty and without burning itself.

3. Take in one hand tube containing broth culture or one containing sterile nutrient broth.

4. Take inoculation loop with other hand and flame the entire wire to redness.

5. Remove the plugs from the tube by grasping them between the fingers of the hand holding the inoculation instrument.

6. Be careful not to bring plugs near to the Bunsen burner.

7. Flame the mouth of broth tubes, insert inoculating loop into the culture and obtaining loopful of inoculums.

8. Introduce the inoculum in to the tube of sterile medium by immersing the loop full of culture in broth.

9. In removing the inoculation loop touch it to the inner surface of tube to remove any left out inoculum.

10. Flame the mouth of the tube again and replace the plugs in the respective tubes.

11. Flame the inoculating loop again to redness to put the loop down and label the tube with microbes used, date your name and initials.

12. Incubate at room temperature for 48 hours.

B. AGAR SLANT TRANSFER:

1. Take in one hand tube containing agar slant, one tube containing sterile nutrient broth. Carry out preliminary steps flaming of inoculating needles, removing plugs, and flaming the mouth of the tube.

2. Insert the inoculating needle into the tube containing agar slant culture and obtaining inoculum by removing a small portion of surface growth.

3. Do not dig into the agar slant, immerse the inoculum into the tube of nutrient broth medium and gently shake the inoculating media to free the microbes adhering to it.

4. Flame the mouth of the tubes and replace the plugs in to the respective tubes.

5. Flame the inoculating loop again to redness to put the loop down and label the tube with microbes used, date your name and initials.

6. Incubate at room temperature for 48 hours.

C. LOOP TRANSFER:

1. Take one tube containing the broth culture and sterile nutrient agar slant grasp them.

2. Carry out preliminary aseptic steps of flaming and plug removal as described previously.

3. Flame the inoculation loop as described previously and remove the inoculum from the culture tube.

4. Place the loop down on the surface of the agar slant at the bottom of the tube.

5. Flame the mouth of the tube and replace the cotton plugs.

6. Flame the inoculation loop and label the freshly inoculated tube.

7. Repeat this procedure and incubate the tubes at room temperature for 48 hours.

Precautions:

1. When using culture media always label or identify the container with the specimen details before inoculation.

2. Inoculate the medium using aseptic techniques and incubate under the appropriate conditions.

CHAPTER NINE

Objective no – 09: To Perform the Gram's staining Method for Bacterial Culture

Gram staining is a differential bacterial staining technique used to differentiate bacteria into Gram-Positive and Gram-Negative types according to their cell wall composition. This technique was introduced in 1884 by the Danish Bacteriologist Hans Christian Gram (1853 September 13 to 1938 November 14). He developed this staining technique to identify bacteria causing pneumonia. Later it became a popular method to classify bacteria into Gram Positive and Gram-Negative types. Bacteria are microscopic organisms that cannot be seen with unaided eye. They can be seen even in unstained preparations such as a wet mount or hanging drop preparation but the morphology is not clear. Bacteria are colourless and when suspended in saline they don't offer any contrast. Besides, bacterial motility makes it difficult to observe the morphology clearly. Hence, bacteria have to be stained to observe them. The dyes often used are toxic chemicals that kill the bacteria. The process of smearing, fixing, and drying often kill the bacteria. This process fixes the bacteria to the slide and their position on slide remains unaltered.

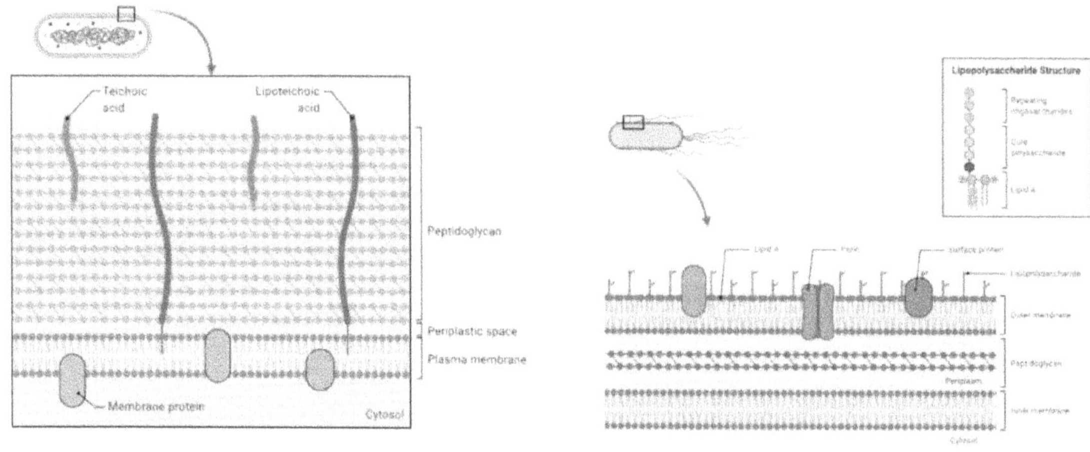

Gram-Positive Bacteria Cell Wall Structure　　**Gram-Negative Bacteria Cell Wall Structure**

Structural Differentiation between Gram Positive and Gram Negative Bacterial Cell Wall

Gram Stain Slide Preparation

1. Take a clean, clear, grease-free glass slide.
2. Sterilize the inoculating loop by flaming and transfer a loop full of bacterial culture suspension in the middle of the glass slide.If culture is on a petri dish or slant, place a drop of water in the middle of the glass slide and using a sterile loop, transfer a small amount of colony and suspend with the water drop.
3. Spread the suspension with the sterile inoculating loop to prepare a thin smear. The smear must not be too thin or too thick.

4. Let the smear air dry and fix it by passing over the flame. Fixing should be done over a gentle flame. Slide must be moved up and down or circularly over the flame to prevent from overheating. Flaming will fix the bacterial cells on the slide and prevent them from washing out.

Procedure:

1. Flood crystal violet solution over fixed smear.
2. After 30 – 60 seconds, pour off the CV solution and rinse with gentle running water.
3. Flood the Gram's Iodine solution over the smear.
4. Leave the iodine solution for 30 – 60 seconds and pour off the excess iodine and rinse with gentle running water.
5. Shake off the excess water over the smear.
6. Decolorize the smear by passing the decolorizing solution till the solution runs down in clear form. Alternatively, add a few drops of decolorizing solution and shake gently and rinse with distilled water after 5 seconds.
7. Rinse with distilled water to wash decolorizer.
8. Shake off the excess water over the smear.
9. Pour counter stain over the smear.
10. Leave for 30 – 60 seconds and wash with gentle running water.
11. Air dry or blow-dry the smear.

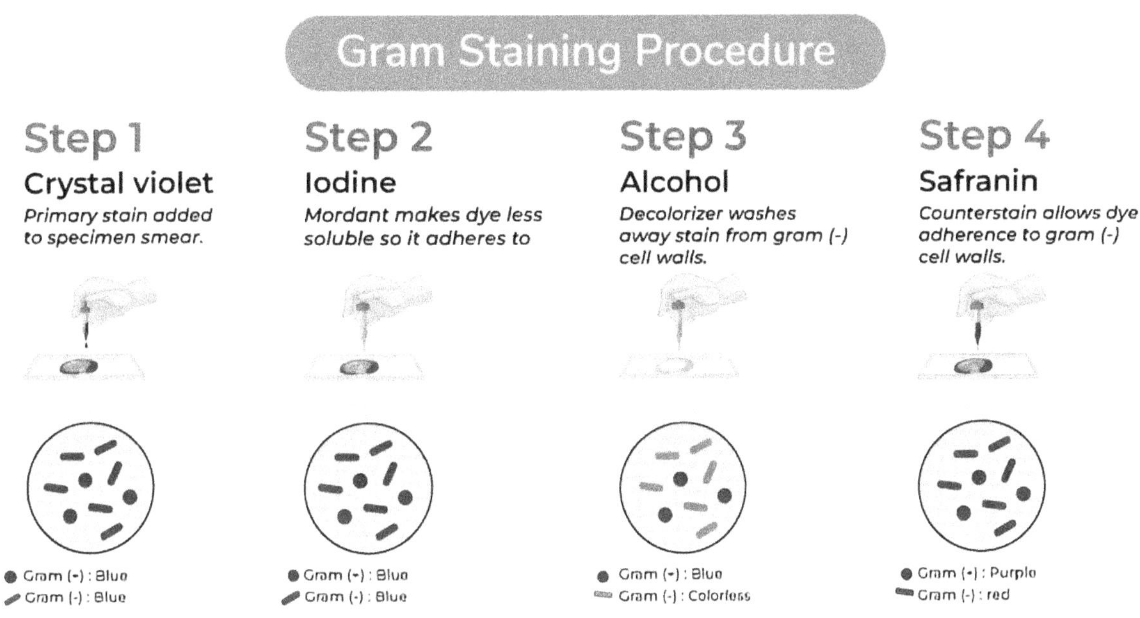

Procedure of Gram's Staining

Results:

• Gram-Positive bacteria appear violet or purple.
• Gram-Negative bacteria appear pink or red.

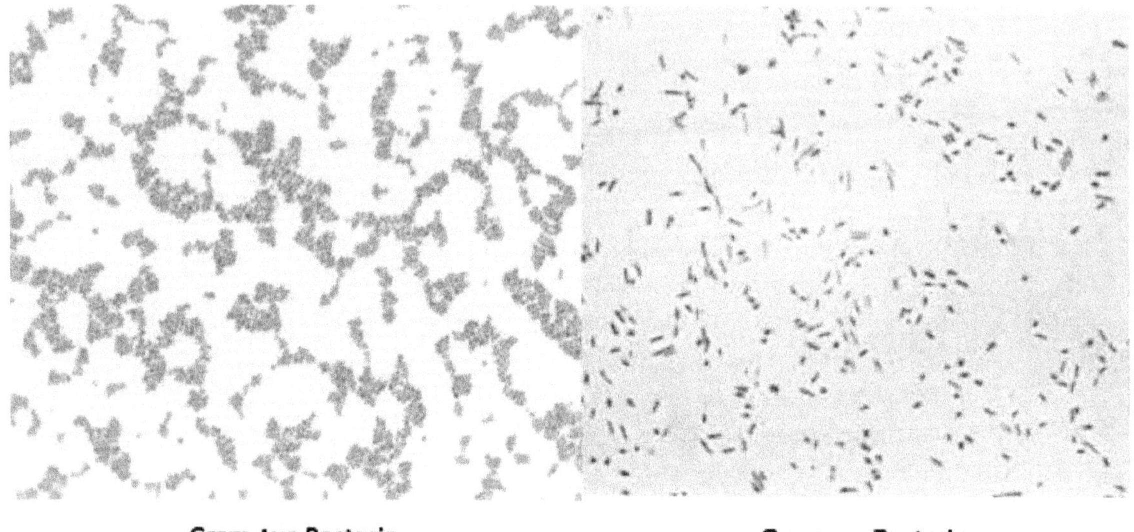

Gram +ve Bacteria　　　　**Gram -ve Bacteria**

Results of Gram`s Staining

Examples of Gram-positive bacteria:

1. **Gram-positive cocci–**_Staphylococcus spp., Streptococcus spp., Enterococcus spp.,_ etc.
2. **Gram-positive bacilli–** _Bacillus spp., Clostridium spp., Lactobacillus spp., Streptomyces spp._ and other Actinobacteria, _Listeria spp., Corynebacterium spp.,_ etc.

Examples of Gram-Negative bacteria:

1. **Gram negative cocci–** _Neisseria spp., Moraxella spp., Acinetobacter spp._ etc
2. **Gram negative bacilli-**_E. coli, Klebsiella spp., Salmonella spp., Shigella spp., Pseudomonas spp., Proteus spp.,_ etc.

Precautions:

1. Wear a face mask and gloves before performing the test.
2. Perform the preparation of the smear under the biosafety cabinet.
3. After preparation of the smear, you must fix the sample. The bacteria will wash off the slide during staining if you do not fix them to the slide.
4. If you heat fix too little, the bacteria will wash off the slide. If you heat fix too much, you will cook the bacteria and denature them.
5. Decontaminate the material by autoclaving after the completion of testing.

CHAPTER TEN

Objective no – 10: To Perform Simple Staining for Bacteria

Its principle is based on producing a **marked contrast** between the **organism** and its surroundings by using basic stain. A basic dye consists of a positive **chromophore**, which strongly attracts the negative cell components and charged molecules like nucleic acids and proteins. Thus, a simple staining technique results in a colored bacterial cell against a colourless background.

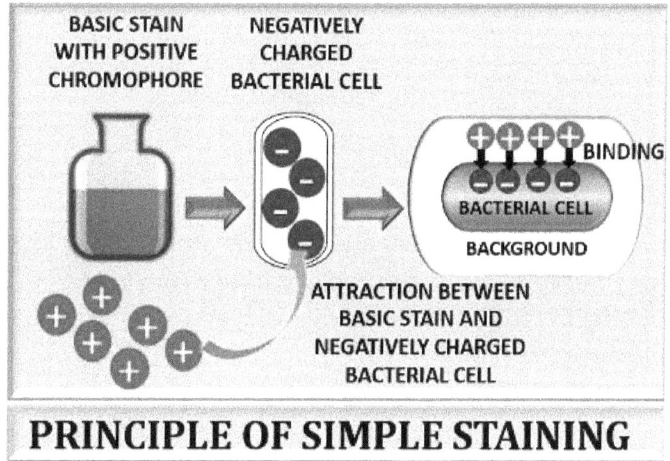

Principal of Simple Staining

Requirement:

Microscope, Methylene blue, crystal violet, and carbol fuchsin, Micro incinerator or Bunsen burner, inoculating loop, staining tray, lens paper, bibulous (highly absorbent) paper, and glass slides

Procedure:

It involves the following three steps:

1. Smear preparation
2. Heat fixing
3. Staining

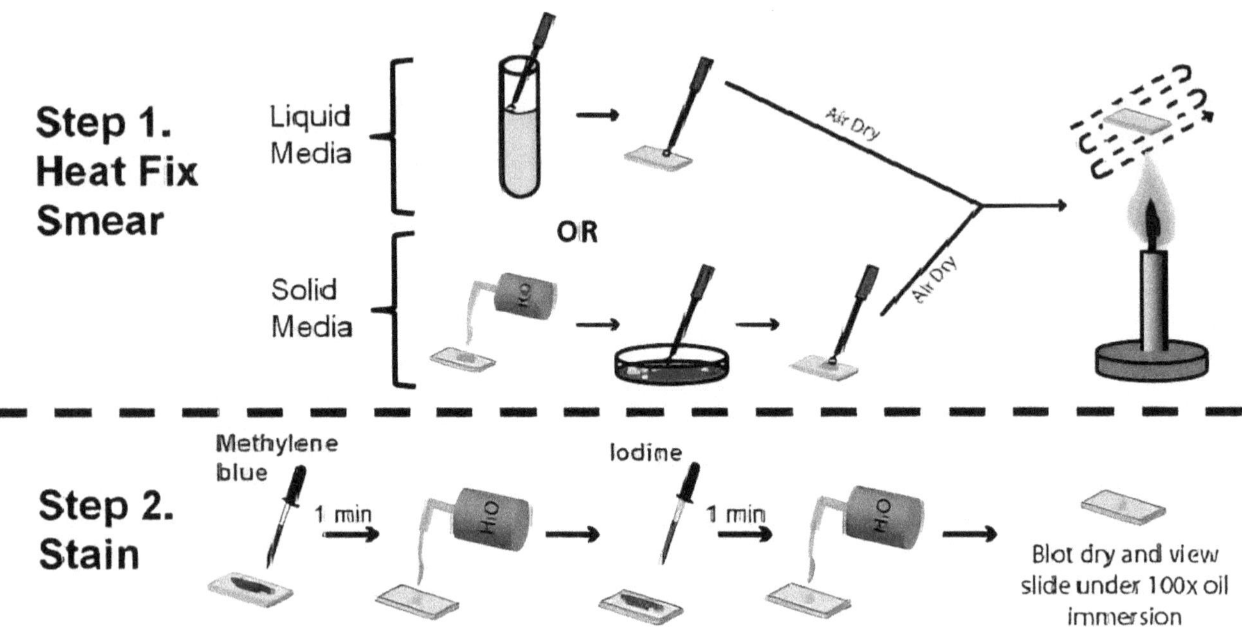

Procedure of Simple Staining

Preparation of a smear:

1. Using a sterilized inoculating loop, transfer a loopful of liquid suspension containing bacteria to a slide (clean grease-free microscopic slide) or transfer an isolated colony from a culture plate to a slide with a water drop.
2. Disperse the bacteria on the loop in the drop of water on the slide and spread the drop over an area the size of a dime. It should be a thin, even smear.
3. Allow the smear to dry thoroughly.
4. Heat-fix the smear cautiously by passing the underside of the slide through the burner flame two or three times. It fixes the cell in the slide. Do not overheat the slide as it will distort the bacterial cells.

Staining

1. Cover the smear with methylene blue and allow the dye to remain in the smear for approximately one minute (Staining time is not critical here; somewhere between 30 seconds to 2 minutes should give you an acceptable stain, the longer you leave the dye in it, the darker will be the stain).
2. Using distilled water wash bottle, gently wash off the excess methylene blue from the slide by directing a gentle stream of water over the surface of the slide.
3. Wash off any stain that got on the bottom of the slide as well.
4. Saturate the smear again but this time with Iodine. Iodine will set the stain.
5. Wash any excess iodine with gently running tap water. Rinse thoroughly. (*You may not get a mention of steps 4 and 5 in some textbooks*)
6. Wipe the back of the slide and blot the stained surface with bibulous paper or with a paper towel.
7. Place the stained smear on the microscope stage smear side up and focus the smear using the 10X objective.
8. Choose an area of the smear in which the cells are well spread in a monolayer. Center the area to be studied, apply immersion oil directly to the smear, and focus the smear under oil with the 100X objective.

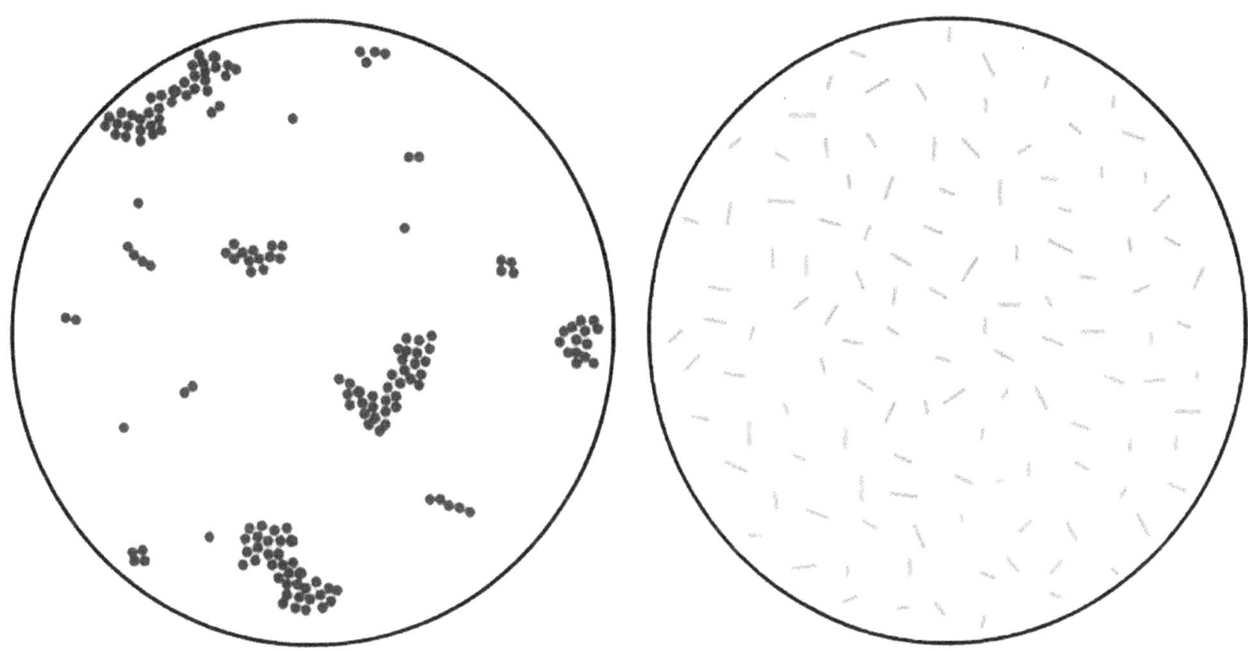

Left: Cocci in Cluster, Right: Bacilli (Image source: *microrao.com*)

Results:

The bacterial cells usually stain uniformly and the color of the cell depends on the type of dye used. If methylene blue is used, some granules in the interior of the cells of some bacteria may appear more deeply stained than the rest of the cell, which is due to the presence of different chemical substances.

Precautions:

1. 1. Clean, dry glass slide must be taken to prepare a smear.
2. Thick dense smears should be avoided.
3. The smear should be properly heat fixed on the slide to avoid its washing off during staining procedure.
4. Do not heat fix in case of negative staining.

CHAPTER ELEVEN

Objective no -11: Hanging Drop Preparation for Motility Study

The hanging drop method is a laboratory technique used to observe the motility of bacteria. It involves suspending a small drop of bacterial culture in a fluid, usually a saline solution, and placing it on a microscope slide with a depression. The cover slip is inverted and placed over the depression, forming a "hanging drop". The hanging drop is then observed under a microscope to observe the motility of the bacterial cells. This preparation gives good views of microbial motility.

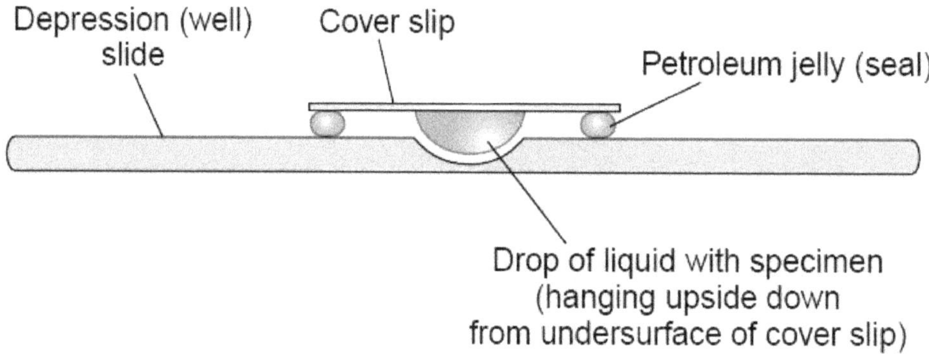

Extracted from: https://microbeonline.com/procedure-hanging-drop-method-test-bacterial-motility/

Requirements:

Microscope,Fresh broth culture of motile bacteria (e.g. Proteus mirabilis), Bunsen burner/spirit lamp, inoculating loop, glass slide (glass slide with depression), cover slip, Paraffin wax.

Principle:

The motility test by hanging drop method is a laboratory technique used to observe the motility of bacteria. The principle behind the hanging drop method is based on the fact that the movement of bacteria can be observed by placing a small drop of bacterial culture on a microscope slide and suspending it over a depression in the slide. The hanging drop is then observed under a microscope to observe the motility of the bacterial cells. The principle of the hanging drop method is based on the physical properties of bacteria and the microscope. Bacteria are small, single-celled organisms that are too small to be seen with the naked eye. To observe bacteria under a microscope, they must be stained or suspended in a solution that makes them visible. However, staining or suspending bacteria can also affect their motility and behavior.

Purpose:

The purpose of the motility test by hanging drop method is to determine the presence or absence of motility in a bacterial culture. The test helps to differentiate between motile and non-motile bacteria, which is a crucial step in the identification of bacterial species.

Procedure:

- Apply petroleum jelly with a cotton swab all the way around the concavity of the depression slide to make a hanging-drop preparation.
- After that, centre a loopful of the culture using sterile procedures on a clean coverslip.
- With the concave surface pointing downward, place the depression slide over the coverslip to cover the culture drop.
- Gently press the slide to seal it to the coverslip. Turn the slide right side up quickly to ensure that the drop sticks to the coverslip's inside surface.
- Start by focusing on the drop culture with the low-power objective, then dim the light source by adjusting the Abbé condenser to study the preparation under a microscope.
- Repeat the inspection using the high-power objective.
- Finally, note down observations in your record.

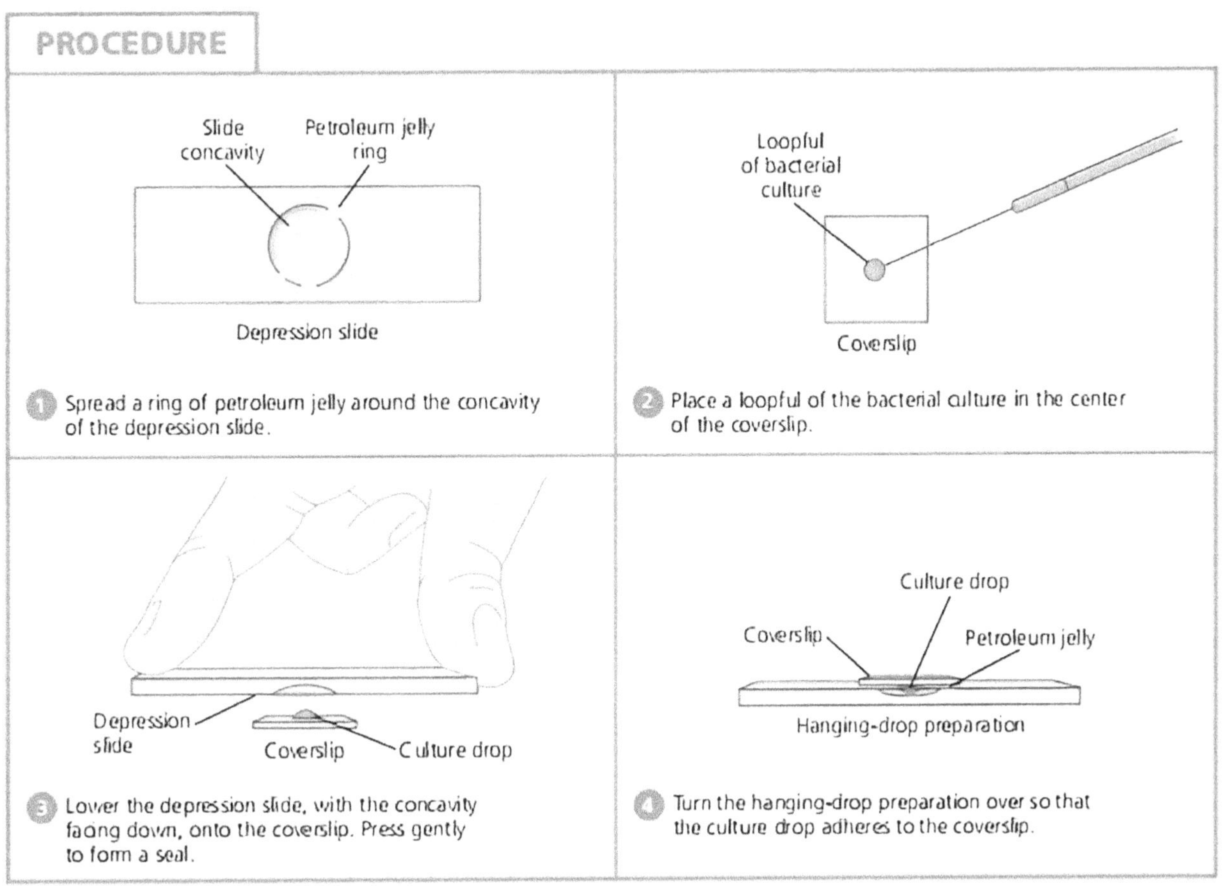

Extracted from : Cappuccino, J. G., & Welsh, C. (2020). Microbiology: A laboratory manual. Pearson.

Observation and Interpretation:

After the hanging drop has been prepared, it should be examined under a microscope to observe bacterial motility. The hanging drop method allows for the observation of live bacteria in a natural state, which can provide valuable information about the bacteria's motility.

Examination of the hanging drop under a microscope:

The hanging drop should be examined under a microscope immediately after preparation to observe bacterial motility. A microscope with a high magnification and good resolution should be used to observe the bacteria. The hanging drop should be viewed under both bright field and dark field microscopy to enhance the visibility of the bacteria.

Interpretation of motility:

The interpretation of motility in the hanging drop method is based on the observation of the movement of bacteria within the bacterial suspension.

Positive motility

Positive motility is observed when bacteria move actively in the bacterial suspension. The movement can be seen as a rapid, continuous, and smooth motion of the bacteria. The bacteria may exhibit a variety of motility patterns such as tumbling, darting, or swarming. The presence of positive motility can indicate the presence of motile bacterial species.

Negative motility

Negative motility is observed when bacteria do not show any movement or appear to be stationary in the bacterial suspension. The bacteria may be immobile, or they may exhibit Brownian motion, which is a random movement caused by the bombardment of water molecules. The absence of motility can indicate the presence of non-motile bacterial species.

In some cases, the hanging drop method may not be sufficient to detect bacterial motility. In these cases, other tests such as the flagella staining or the motility agar test may be used to confirm the presence or absence of bacterial motility.

Note: It is important to observe the hanging drop immediately after preparation, as bacterial motility can decrease over time.

Precautions:

1. The usage of PPE (Gloves, Mask, Lab coat / Gown, Safety goggles, etc.) is required because you will be handling highly infectious, live microorganisms.
2. Use the early culture of the organism, as the organisms are most likely dead in the older cultures.
3. Place a drop of sufficient size on the cover glass; it should not be too large or too small and should hang freely in the depression slide's concavity.
4. Observe first with low power goals, then transition to high power and oil immersion objectives for simple observations.
5. It is important to observe the hanging drop immediately after preparation, as bacterial motility can decrease over time.

CHAPTER TWELVE

Objective no – 12: Biochemical Identification of Bacteria by Indole Test

The indole test is a biochemical test which detects the ability of organisms (bacteria) to produce indole as a metabolic product utilizing tryptophan. The indole test screens for the ability of an organism to degrade the amino acid tryptophan and produce indole. It is used as part of the IMViC procedures, a battery of tests designed to distinguish among members of the family Enterobacteriaceae.

This test demonstrate the ability of certain bacteria to decompose the amino acid tryptophane to indole, which accumulates in the medium. Indole production test is important in the identification of Enterobacteria. Most strains of E. coli, P. vulgaris, P. rettgeri, M. morgani and Providencia species break down the amino acid tryptophan with the release of indole. This is performed by a chain of a number of different intracellular enzymes, a system generally referred to as "tryptophanase." It is used as part of the IMViC procedures,a tests designed to distinguish among members of the family Enterobacteriaceae.

Requirements:

Indole Spot Reagent, Indole Kovacs Reagent

Principle:

Some bacteria can produce an enzyme called 'tryptophanase' which helps them to metabolize the amino acid 'tryptophan' into 'indole, pyruvic acid, and ammonia'. When the indole reagent is added to a medium with a bacterial culture that has produced indole, the indole combines with the aldehyde present in the reagent to give a distinctive color. Test bacteria are cultured in the medium containing tryptophan for 24 – 48 hours and an indole reagent is added following the incubation to read the result. A positive result is indicated by the formation of a pink to violet-red or green to blue color ring according to the type of reagent used. A negative color is indicated by the formation of a lack of color change or a slight yellowish color ring at the top.

Procedure:

1. Take a sterilized test tubes containing 4 ml of tryptophan broth.
2. Inoculate the tube aseptically by taking the growth from 18 to 24 hrs culture.
3. Incubate the tube at 37°C for 24-28 hours.
4. Add 0.5 ml of Kovac's reagent to the broth culture.
5. Observe for the presence or absence of ring.

Indole Spot Reagent (DMACA) Procedure

1. Place several drops of Indole Spot Reagent on a piece of filter paper.
2. With an inoculating loop or wooden applicator stick, pick a portion of an 18–24-hour isolated colony from a non-selective media and rub it onto the reagent saturated area of the filter paper.
3. Examine immediately

Ingredients per liter: *

Indole Spot Reagent:

p-Dimethylaminocinnamaldehyde (DMACA) 10.0 gm, Hydrochloric Acid, 37% 100.0 ml, Deionized Water 900.0 ml.

Indole Kovacs Reagent:

p-Dimethylaminobenzaldehyde 50.0 gm, Hydrochloric Acid, 37% 250.0 ml, Amyl Alcohol 750.0 ml

* Adjusted and/or supplemented as required to meet performance criteria.

Result & Interpretation:

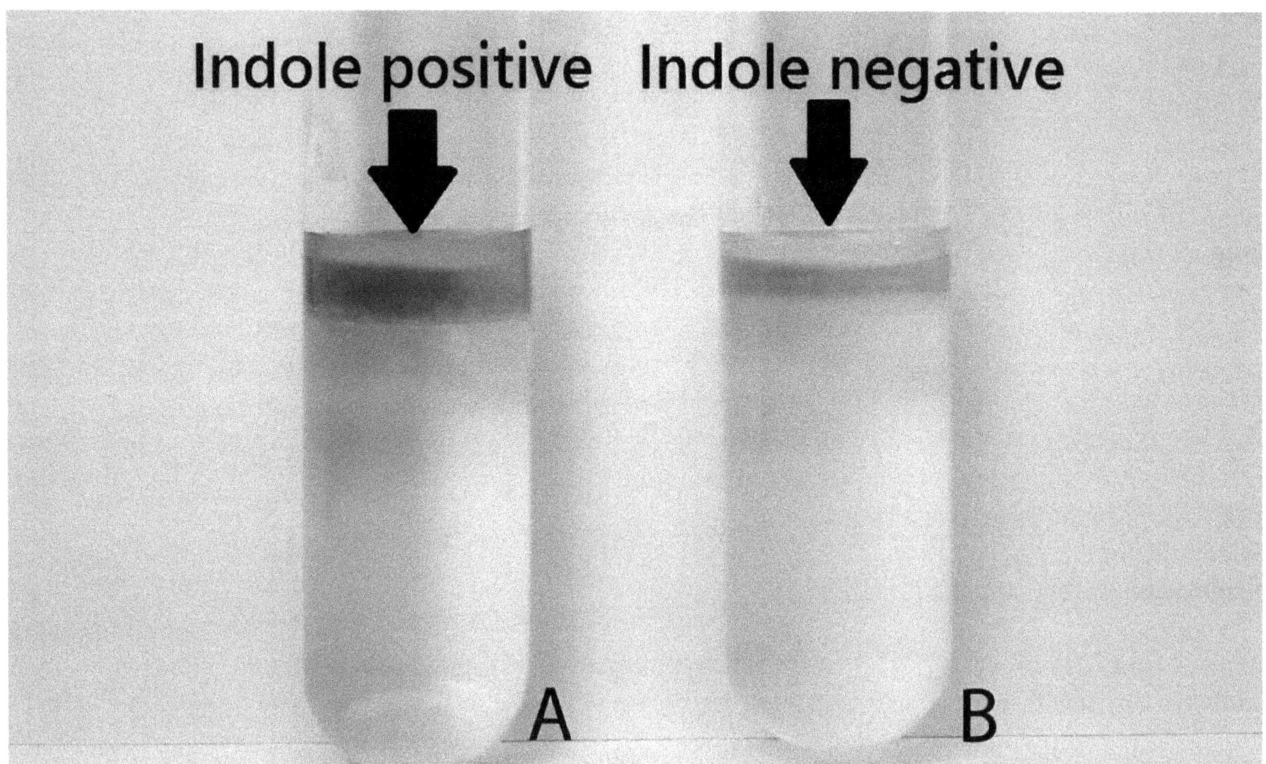

https://microbiologyinfo.com/indole-test-principle-reagents-procedure-result-interpretation-and-limitations/

Positive: Formation of a pink to red color ("cherry-red ring") in the reagent layer on top of the medium within seconds of adding the reagent.

Examples: *Escherichiacoli, Flavobacterium* sp., *Haemophilus influenzae, Klebsiella oxytoca, Proteus* sp. *Enterococcus faecalis*, and *Vibrio* sp.

Negative: No color change even after the addition of appropriate reagent.

Examples: *Actinobacillus* spp., *Alcaligenes* sp., *Pseudomonas* sp., *Salmonella* sp.

Precautions:

1. Always use the bacteria grown in the tryptophan-rich medium for testing.

2. Read the result within 20 seconds of the addition of the indole reagent.

3. Do not use medium-containing dye/indicators like EMB, McConkey, etc.

CHAPTER THIRTEEN

Objective no – 13: Biochemical identification of bacteria by Methyl Red (MR) Test

The MR test is actually a type of tests that uses broth medium containing glucose to determine the possible types of glucose fermentation being conducted by a bacterial species. Some bacterial species ferment glucose a using mixed acid fermentation pathway. The methyl red test is used to detect the ability of an organism to produce and maintain acid end products from glucose fermentation. The test is useful for differentiating among members of the Enterobacteriaceae, and is usually performed alongside the Voges-Proskauer (VP) test since both test are performed on cultures grown in MRVP Broth. The methyl red test is a quantitative test that measures the amount of acid produced by different bacterial species. All members of the Enterobacteriaceae can convert glucose to pyruvic acid by the Embden-Meyerhof pathway, but bacteria can further metabolize pyruvic acid by two different pathways.

Requirements:

MR broth (Buffered peptone 7.0 gm/L, Dextrose 5.0 gm/L, Dipotassium phosphate 5.0 gm/L, Final pH (at 25°C) pH 6.9±0.2), Methyl red solution, 0.02%

Principle:

Some bacteria have the ability to utilize glucose and convert it to a stable acid like lactic acid, acetic acid or formic acid as the end product.These bacteria initially metabolise glucose to pyruvic acid, which is further metabolized through the 'mixed acid pathway to produce the stable acid. The type of acid produced differs from species to species and depends on the specific enzymatic pathways present in the bacteria. The acid so produced decreases the pH to 4.5 or below, which is indicated by a change in the color of methyl red from yellow to red.

In the methyl red test (MR test), the test bacteria is grown in a broth medium containing glucose. If the bacteria has the ability to utilise glucose with production of a stable acid, the color of the methyl red changes from yellow to red, when added into the broth culture.

Media and Reagents used in Methyl Red (MR) Test

MRVP broth (pH 6.9)

Ingredients per liter of deionized water:

buffered peptone= 7.0 gm

glucose= 5.0 gm

dipotassium phosphate= 5.0 gm

Methyl red solution, 0.02%

a. Dissolve 0.1 g of methyl red in 300 ml of ethyl alcohol, 95%.

b. Add sufficient distilled water to make 500 ml.

c. Store at 4 to 8 degree C in a brown bottle. Solution is stable for 1 year.

Procedure:

1. Prior to inoculation, allow medium to equilibrate to room temperature.

2. Using organisms taken from an 18-24 hour pure culture, lightly inoculate the medium.

3. Incubate aerobically at 37 degrees C. for 24 hours.

4. Following 24 hours of incubation, aliquot 1ml of the broth to a clean test tube.

5. Reincubate the remaining broth for an additional 24 hours.

6. Add 2 to 3 drops of methyl red indicator to aliquot.

7. Observe for red color immediately.

Result & Interpretation:

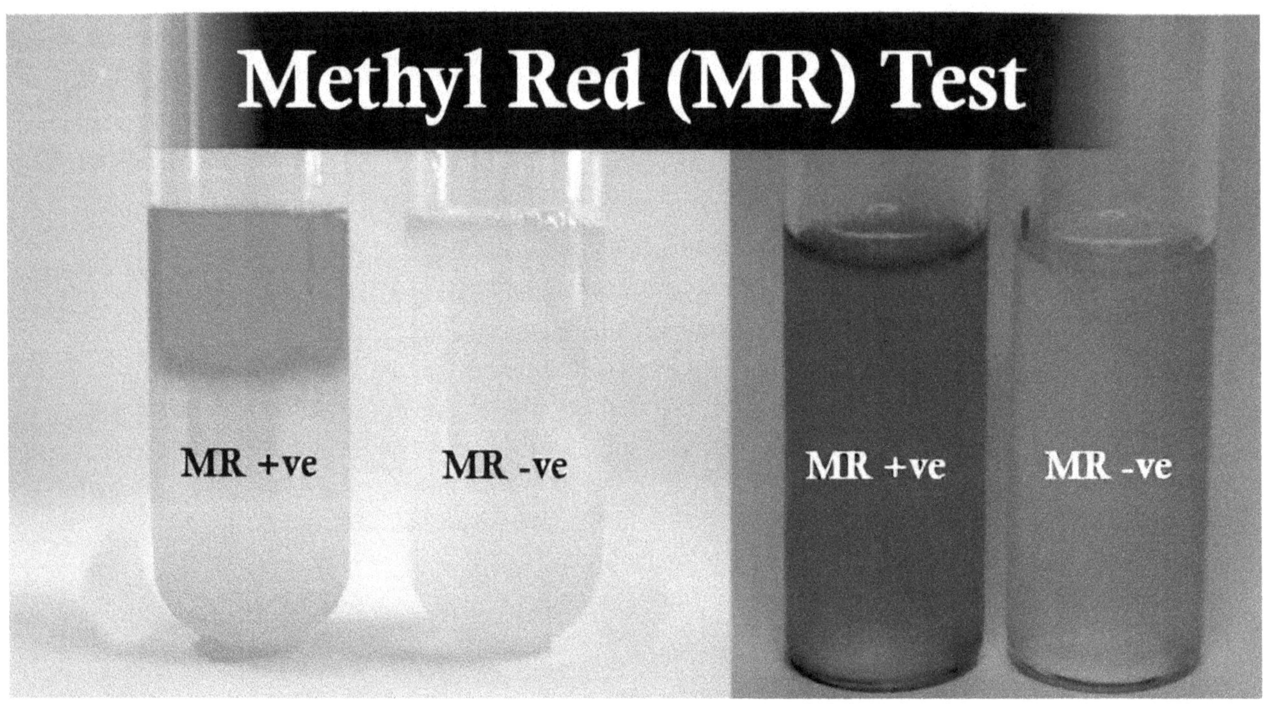

https://microbenotes.com/methyl-red-mr-test-objectives-principle-media-used-procedure-result-interpretation-limitations-and-examples/

MR Positive: Bright red color

Examples: *Escherichia coli* (ATCC25922), Yersinia sps, etc.

Weakly positive: Red-orange color

MR Negative: Yellow color

Examples: Enterobacter aerogenes (ATCC13048), Klebsiella pneumoniae, etc.

Preacautions:

1. Avoid contact: Avoid breathing the vapor and contact with your eyes or skin.

2. Sterilize: Properly sterilize specimens, containers, and media after use to prevent microbiological hazards.

3. Incubation time: The minimum incubation time for the MR broth is 48 hours, but you may need to incubate it for an additional three days if the results are inconclusive.

4. Inoculation: Avoid over-inoculating the MR-VP broth, and standardize the inoculum used for optimal results.

5. Reagents: The reagents used can irritate or burn your skin, so use appropriate handling procedures.

CHAPTER FOURTEEN

Objective no – 14: Biochemical identification of bacteria by Vogus Proskauer (VP) Test

Voges and Proskauer, in 1898, first observed the production of a red color after the addition of potassium hydroxide to cultures grown on specific media. Harden later revealed that the development of the red color was a result of acetyl-methyl carbinol production. In 1936, Barrit made the test more sensitive by adding alpha-naphthol to the medium before adding potassium hydroxide.

Requipments:

Test tubes. Incubator, dropper, autoclave, bunsen burner, inoculating loop Weighing Machine, MRVP broth (pH 6.9, Buffered peptone (7.0 gm), Glucose (5.0 gm), Dipotassium phosphate (5.0 gm), Barritt's Reagent A (Alpha-Naphthol 5% 50 gm, Absolute Ethanol 1000 ml), Barritt's Reagent B (Potassium Hydroxide 400 gm, Deionized Water 1000 ml)

Principle:

The Voges-Proskauer (VP) test is used to determine if an organism produces acetylmethyl carbinol from glucose fermentation. If present, acetylmethyl carbinol is converted to diacetyl in the presence of $\propto$- naphthol, strong alkali (40% KOH), and atmospheric oxygen. The $\propto$-naphthol was not part of the original procedure but was found to act as a color intensifier by Barritt and must be added first. The diacetyl and quanidine-containing compounds found in the peptones of the broth then condense to form a pinkish red polymer.

$$2 \text{ pyruvate} = \text{acetoin} + 2CO2$$
$$\text{acetoin} + NADH + H+ = 2,3\text{-butanediol} + NAD+$$

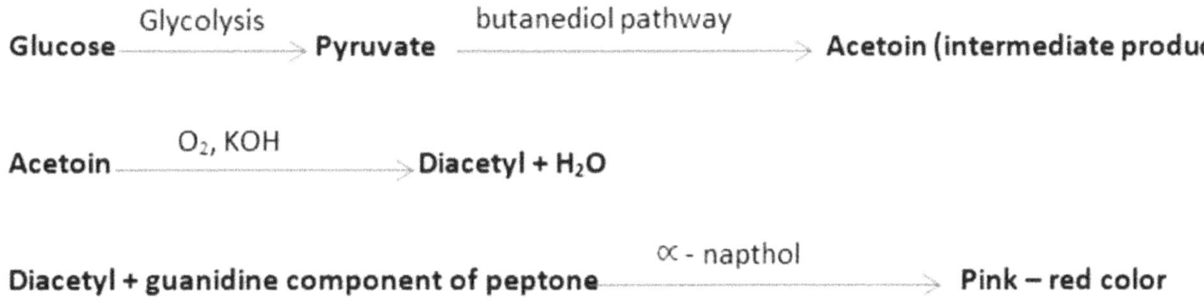

Reaction Mcchanism for VP Test

Procedure:

- Using a sterile inoculating loop, pick up well-isolated colonies of sample bacteria from 18 to 24 hours old culture and inoculate the broth.
- Incubate the tubes aerobically for 18 to 24 hours at 35±2°C.
- Following incubation, transfer 2 mL of broth to a clean (sterile if possible) test tube.

- Add 6 drops of Reagent A (5% α-naphthol solution) and mix properly by shaking.
- Add 2 drops of Reagent B (40% KOH solution) and mix properly by shaking.
- Observe for the formation of red-pink color at the surface of the medium within 30 minutes. Continuously shake the tube vigorously during the 30-minute waiting period.

If no color is developed (negative reaction) re-incubate the remaining broth for additional 24 hours and test again.

Results & Interpretation:

- **A positive result** is indicated by the **formation of a pink-red color** over the surface of the
- medium.
- **A negative result** is indicated by a **lack of pink-red color** over the surface of the medium or the formation of the copper color.

Precautions:

1. Over-inoculation results in inhibited bacterial growth; hence, it is better to limit the bacterial inoculum to less than 10^9 cells per mL of broth.

2. Use freshly prepared reagents. If reagents need to be stored, always store them in a dark place.

3. Mix the medium and reagent properly by shaking vigorously so that oxygen dissolves properly.

4. Wait up to 30 minutes after the addition of reagents while shaking continuously before reporting negative.

5. Prohibit over-incubation (incubation more than 3 days) because it can give a weak or false negative reaction.

6. An excessive amount of KOH gives a weakly positive reaction, so use the reagents in the appropriate amount.

CHAPTER FIFTEEN

Objective no – 15: Biochemical identification of bacteria by Citrate Utilisation

The citrate test detects the ability of an organism to use citrate as the sole source of carbon and energy. All living things need carbon to survive. The carbon-containing molecules that bacteria can utilize as a carbon source differs based on the bacterial species and is dependent on their genes. Their genes dictate what enzymes the bacterial species can produce. Since enzymes are necessary for a cell's metabolic reactions, the genes of a bacterial species dictate their abilities to use different carbon sources.

Some bacterial species, but not all bacterial species, can utilize citrate as a source of carbon. Organisms that can survive using citrate as the sole source of carbon have a citrate permease enzyme that can transport citrate molecules into the cell. The citrate is then made into pyruvate, which can be converted into a variety of different products in the cell.

Requirements:
Inoculating loops or needles, Incubator, Simmon's Citrate Agar, Christensen's citrate sulfide medium

Principle:
The citrate test is performed to differentiate Gram-negative bacilli of the Enterobacteriaceae family. It is an important test that allows the species-level identification of the members of the Enterobacteriaceae family.

- Citrate agar is used to test the ability of an organism to utilize citrate as a source of energy.
- The agar medium contains citrate as the sole carbon source and inorganic ammonium salts as the sole source of nitrogen.
- The growth of the organism is indicative of the utilization of citrate as it is an intermediate metabolite in the Krebs cycle. The enzyme citrase breaks down citrate into oxaloacetate and acetate, where oxaloacetate is further broken down to form pyruvate and carbon dioxide.
- The release of carbon dioxide induces the metabolism of ammonium salts, causing the formation of ammonia or sodium carbonate, both of which increase the alkalinity of the medium.
- The shift in pH turns the bromthymol blue indicator in the medium from green to blue above pH 7.6

$$\text{Citrate} \rightarrow \text{Oxaloacetic acid} \rightarrow \text{Pyruvic acid} + CO_2$$
$$\textbf{Excess of sodium from sodium citrate} + CO_2 + H_2O \rightarrow Na_2CO_3$$

- The growth of the organism on the medium followed by the change in the color; as a result, of citrate metabolism gives a positive citrate test.

Procedure:
1. Streak the slant back and forth with a light inoculum picked from the center of a well-isolated colony.
2. Incubate aerobically at 35 to 37C for up to 4-7 days.
3. Observe a color change from green to blue along the slant.
A positive test is demonstrated by growth with a color change from green to intense blue along the slant.

Positive Reaction: Growth with color change from green to intense blue along the slant.

Examples: *Salmonella, Edwardsiella, Citrobacter, Klebsiella, Enterobacter, Serratia, Providencia,* etc.

A negative test is demonstrated by no growth and no color change, and the color of the slant remains green.

Negative Reaction: No growth and No color change; Slant remains green.

Examples: *Escherichia, Shigella, Morganella, Yersinia* etc.

Precautions:

1. Luxuriant growth on the slant without an accompanying color change may indicate a positive test.

2. Tests with equivocal results should be repeated.

3. The slant should not be stabbed since the test requires an aerobic environment.

CHAPTER SIXTEEN

Objective no – 16: Biochemical identification of bacteria by Oxidase Test

Oxidase test was first introduced by Gordon and McLeod in 1928 to distinguish Neisseria gonorrhoeae from Staphylococcus spp. and Streptococcus spp. Later it was modified by Kovacs and used Kovacs' oxidase reagent (tetra-methyl-p-phenylenediamine dihydrochloride) for the identification of the cytochrome oxidase enzyme. Again, Gaby and Hadley modified the test and used p-amino dimethylaniline oxalate with α-naphthol as a reagent to detect the cytochrome oxidase enzyme in tube culture. The oxidase test is done to find out the presence of a cytochrome oxidase enzyme which will catalyse and transport electrons between electron donors in the bacteria and a redox dye-tetramethyl-p-phenylene-diamine. At the end dye colour changes to a deep purple colour. This test is used in the identification of Pseudomonas, Neisseria, Alcaligens, Aeromonas, based on the production of cytochrome oxidase enzyme.

Requiremnets:

Petri Plates, Whatman no.1 Filter paper (disc or strip), Weighing Machine, Autoclave, Bunsen burner, Test Tubes, Dropper, Inoculating loop (Cotton Swab), PPE Other laboratory materials.

Culture Media and Reagents:

Kovacs Oxidase Reagent: 1% tetra-methyl-p-phenylenediamine dihydrochloride, in water, Gordon and McLeod's Reagent: 1% dimethyl-p-phenylenediamine dihydrochloride, in water, Gaby and Hadley (indophenol oxidase) Reagent:1% α-naphthol in 95% ethano, 1% p-aminodimethylaniline, HCL

Composition of Nutrient Broth per 1000 mL:

Peptone........................... 5.00 grams

HM Peptone B (Beef Extract)................................. 1.50 grams

Yeast Extract................................ 1.50 grams

Sodium Chloride...................................5.00 grams

Final pH 7.4 ± 0.2 at 25°C

Principle:

This test is performed to determine or identify the presence of an enzyme cytochrome oxidase (of the electron transport chain) in bacterial cells. The substrate used is tetramethyl-p-phenylenediamine dihydrochloride, which is oxidized to a purple colored end product called indophenol by the enzyme oxidase. The development of a dark purple color is a positive test that indicates the presence of oxidase, whereas if the enzyme is not present, the reagent remains reduced and is colorless.

Procedure:

(Gordon and McLeod Oxidase Reagent or Kovacs' Oxidase Reagent can be used for oxidase test following the filter paper method, swab method, or direct plate method.

Take 2 to 3 drops of freshly prepared oxidase reagent and place the filter paper in a clean and dry Petri dish.

With the help of glass rod remove a colony of the test organism from culture plate and smeared it on the filter paper and wait.

Observe for the production of a deep purple-blue color within a few seconds.

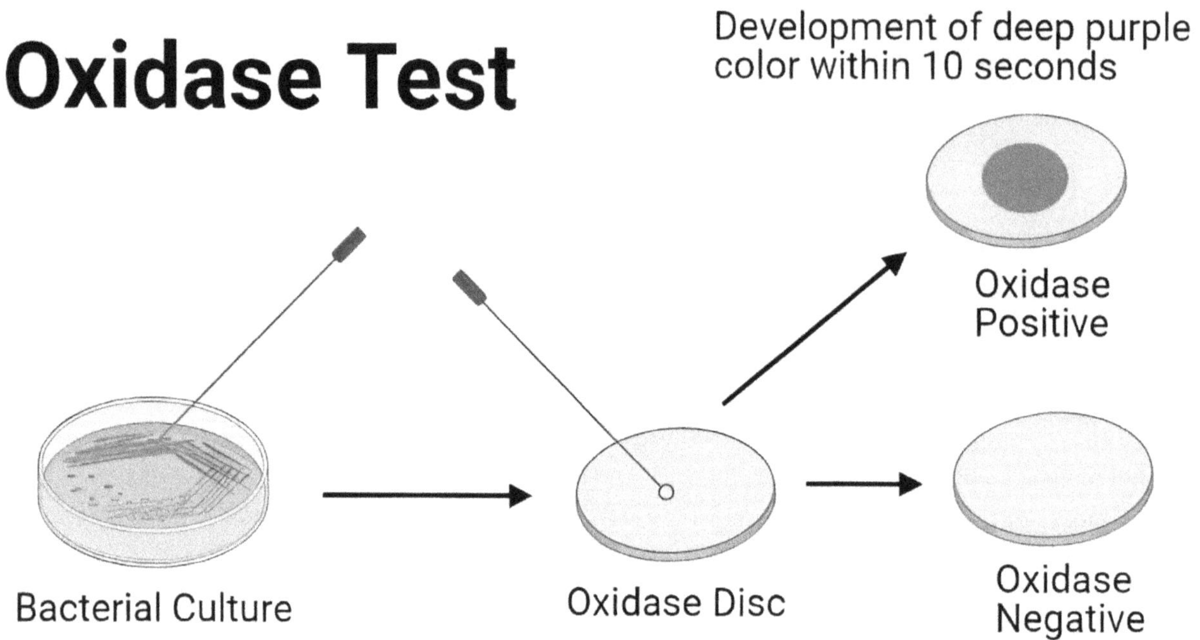

Oxidase Test procedure

Dry Filter Paper Method:

Whatman's No. 1 filter paper is taken and dipped in a freshly prepared solution of 1% of tetramethyl-p-phenylene-diamine dihydrochloride then drained for about 30 seconds, the strips are later freeze dried and finally stored in a dark bottle tightly sealed with a screw cap. While testing, the strip is removed, and are kept in a petri dish and sprayed with distilled water. A platinum loop is used to pick up the colony and smear over the moist area. intense deep-purple hue, appearing within 5-10 seconds, indicates its positive reaction, absence of colouration or by colouration later than 60 seconds is a negative reaction. The oxidase reagents are actually unstable and need to be freshly prepared for use, so this method was found to be convenient.

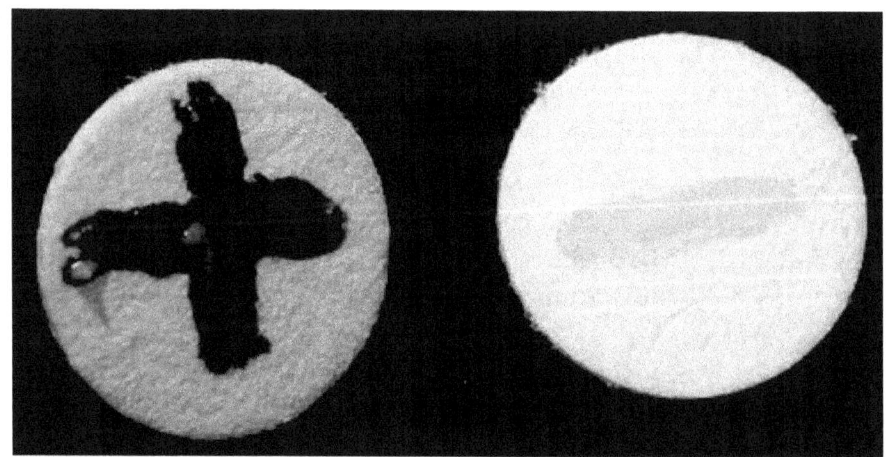

Oxidase-positive Pseudomonas aeruginosa (left) and oxidase-negative Escherichia coli (right). source microbes online.com

Results:

Oxidase positive: color changes to dark purple within 5 to 10 seconds.

Delayed oxidase-positive: color changes to purple within 60 to 90 seconds.

Oxidase negative: color does not change or it takes longer than 2 minutes.

Wet Filter Paper Method:

Filter paper strips are soaked in a freshly made 1% solution of the reagent. The platinum loop is rubbed on the culture. Intense deep-purple hue, appearing within 5-10 seconds is indication of positive reaction and absence of colouration is a negative reaction.

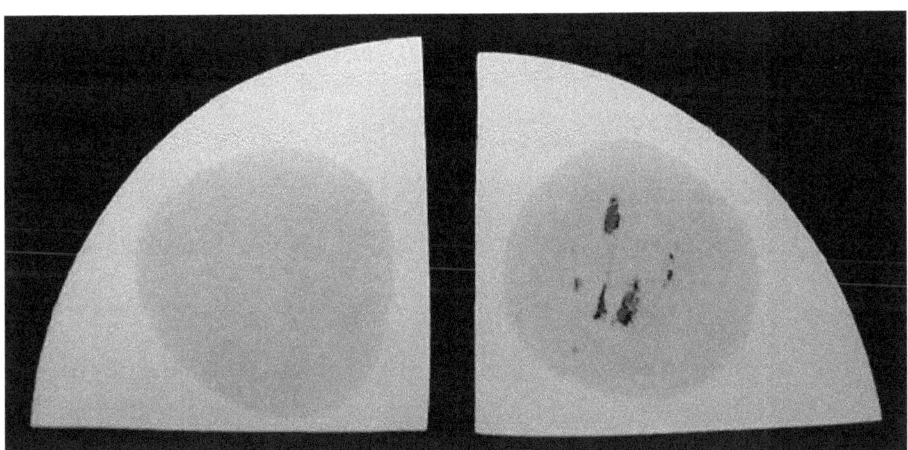

The filter paper on the left-hand is negative while the filter paper on the right-hand side is positive as indicated by the blue colour. source: https://www.microbiologyclass.com

Results:

Oxidase positive: color changes to dark purple within 5 to 10 seconds.

Delayed oxidase-positive: color changes to purple within 60 to 90 seconds.

Oxidase negative: color does not change or it takes longer than 2 minutes.

Swab Method:

Moisten a sterile swab with 1% Kovacs' oxidase reagent.

Touch a well-isolated colony from a fresh culture with the swab.

Observe the development of color in the swab and note the time required for change in color for up to 60 seconds.

Direct Plate Method:

Grow a fresh culture (18 to 24 hours) of bacteria on nutrient agar or trypticase soy agar using the streak plate method so that well-isolated colonies are present.

Place 1 or 2 drops of 1% Kovács oxidase reagent on the organisms.

Do not invert or flood plate.

Observe for color changes.

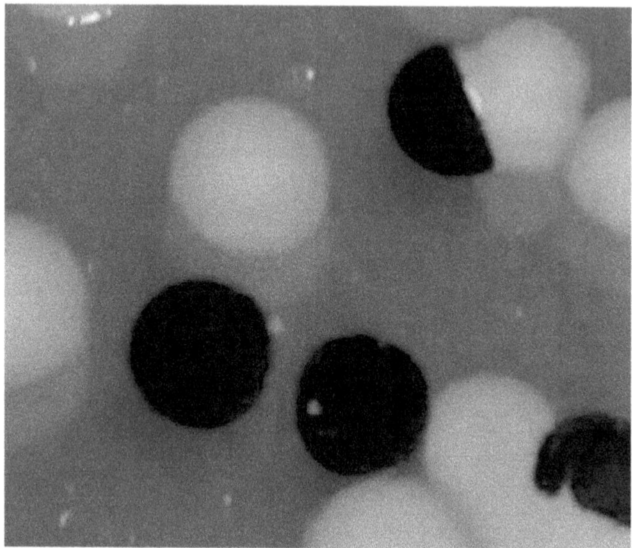

Oxidase-positive Vibrio cholerae showing purple colonies, and oxidase-negative Escherichia coli with lack of color change

Results:

Oxidase positive: color changes to dark purple within 5 to 10 seconds.

Delayed oxidase-positive: color changes to purple within 60 to 90 seconds.

Oxidase negative: color does not change or it takes longer than 2 minutes.

Test Tube Method:

Grow a fresh culture (18 to 24 hours) of bacteria in 4.5 ml of nutrient broth (or standard media that does not contain a high concentration of sugar).

Add 0.2 ml of 1% α-naphthol, then add 0.3 ml of 1% paminodimethylaniline oxalate (Gaby and Hadley reagents). Observe for color changes.

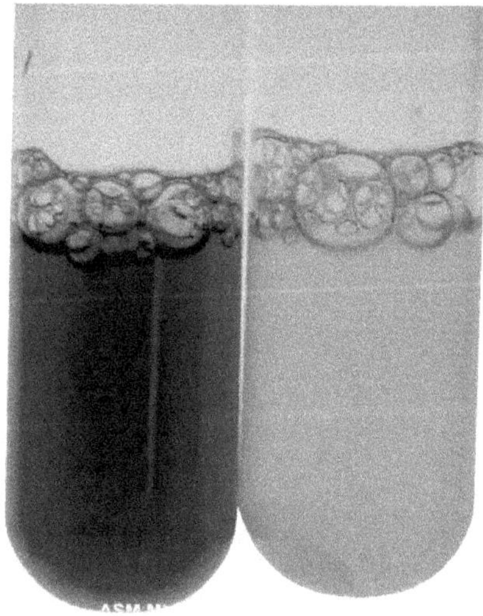

Oxidase positive Neisseria sicca (left) and oxidase negative Staphylococcus aureus (right)

Results:

Positive Test

1. Development of purple to deep blue color within 10 to 30 seconds indicates a positive oxidase test.
2. Development of purple to deep blue color within 30 to 60 seconds indicates a weak oxidase positive reaction or delayed oxidase positive.

Negative Test

1. No development of purple to deep blue color within 60 seconds.
2. Development of purple to deep blue color after 60 seconds.

Quality Control:
Bacterial species showing positive and negative reactions should be run as controls at frequent intervals. The following are suggested:
A. Oxidase positive: Pseudomonas aeruginosa
B. Oxidase negative: Escherichia coli

Precautions:
1. Timing is critical to accurate testing.
2. Use fresh reagents, no older than 1 week, older reagents can autooxidize thus giving erroneous results.
3. Do not use if the reagent or filter paper is purple.
4. Do not test organisms growing on media that contain glucose or dyes (e.g., MacConkey agar or EMB agar).
5. Do not use nickel-base alloy wires containing chromium and iron (nichrome) to pick the colony and make a smear as this may give false-positive results.
6. Bacteria grown on media-containing dyes may give aberrant results.
7. Older cultures are less metabolically active so may give false-negative results within the mentioned observation time.

CHAPTER SEVENTEEN

Objective no – 17: Biochemical identification of bacteria by Catalase Test

The catalase test helps the detection of the enzyme catalase in bacteria. It is essential for separating catalase-positive Micrococcaceae from catalase negative Streptococcaceae. While it is actually useful in separating between genera, it is also important in speciation of certain gram positives such as Aerococcus urinae which is gram positive from Aerococcus viridians which is gram negative. Catalase was first observed in 1818 by Louis Jacques Thénard, who discovered (H2O2).

Requirements:

Hydrogen peroxide reagent,30% H2O2 for Neisseria 15% H2O2 for anaerobes, 3% H2O2 for other bacteria, Glass slide, Sterile wooden or glass sticks.

Principle:

The aerobic and facultative anaerobic microorganism's metabolites give rise to toxic by-products like hydrogen peroxide and superoxide radical (O2). These are considered toxic to the organisms and can even result in lysis of cells if not broken down. In the case of pathogenic organisms, they present different mechanisms that break down these products to non-toxic substances. These organisms produce enzymes namely catalase hydrolysis that helps in breaking down hydrogen peroxide into water and gaseous oxygen, that can be confirmed by production of gas bubbles.

The mechanism is given below:

H2O2 ————---------------> H2O + O2

catalase

The main aim of producing catalase enzymes by the organism is to protect itself against the lethal effect of hydrogen peroxide gathering at the end of the aerobic metabolism. To confirm the presence of the catalase enzyme we need to add hydrogen peroxide to the bacterial inoculum, if an oxygen bubble produces it means catalase is present and no bubble means absence of enzyme. This test is used to identify organisms that produce the enzyme, catalase. This enzyme detoxifies hydrogen peroxide by breaking it down into water and oxygen gas. The bubbles resulting from production of oxygen gas clearly indicate a catalase positive result. The sample on the right below is catalase positive. The Staphylococcus spp. and the Micrococcus spp. are catalase positive. The Streptococcus and Enterococcus spp. are catalase negative.

Procedure:

Many methods are available for catalase tests methods like

1. Slide or drop catalase test,

2. Tube method,

3. Heat-stable catalase mainly used for the separation of Mycobacterium species. The semi quantitative catalase for the finding of Mycobacterium tuberculosis. the protocol of slide methods is given below

Tube Method

1. Pour 1-2 ml of hydrogen peroxide solution into a test tube.

2. Using a sterile wooden stick or a glass rod, take several colonies of the 18 to 24 hours test organism and immerse in the hydrogen peroxide solution.
3. Observe for immediate bubbling.

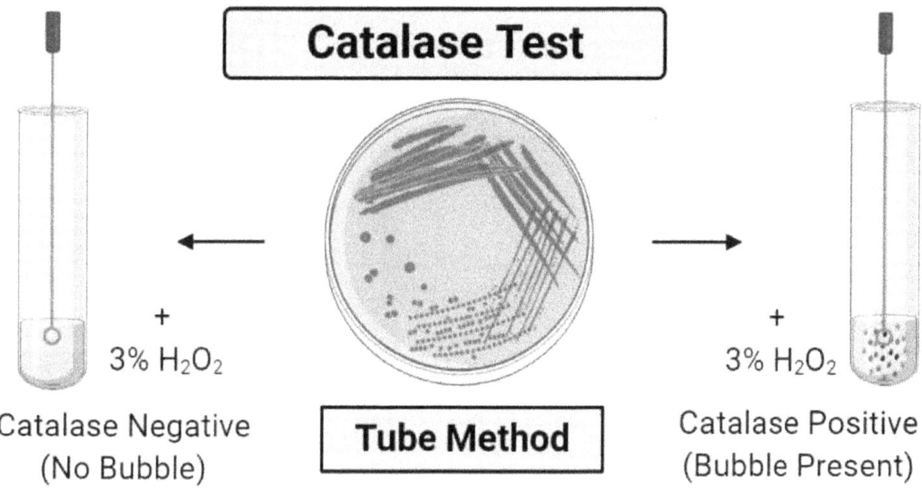

TUBE METHOD

Slide Method

1. Use a loop or sterile wooden stick to transfer a small amount of colony growth in the surface of a clean, dry glass slide.
2. Place a drop of 3% H_2O_2 in the glass slide.
3. Observe for the evolution of oxygen bubbles.

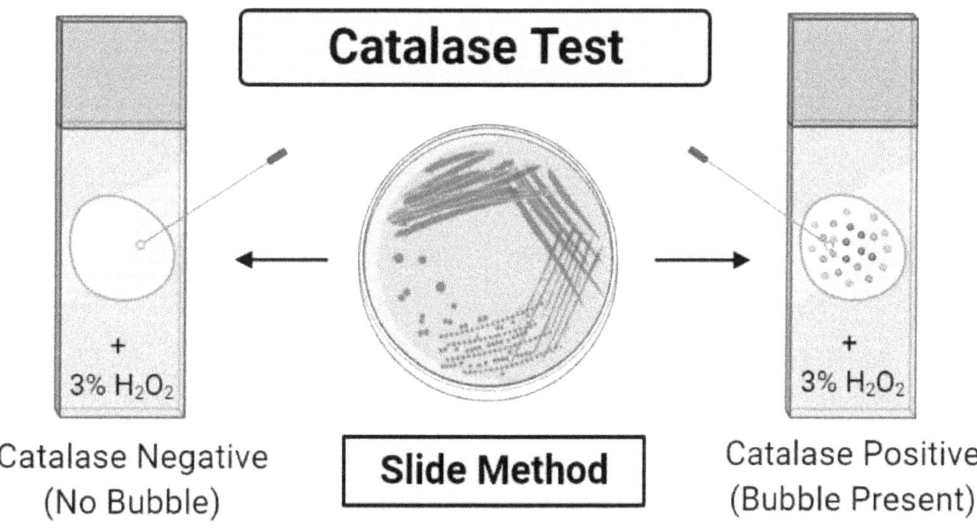

SLIDE METHOD

Results:

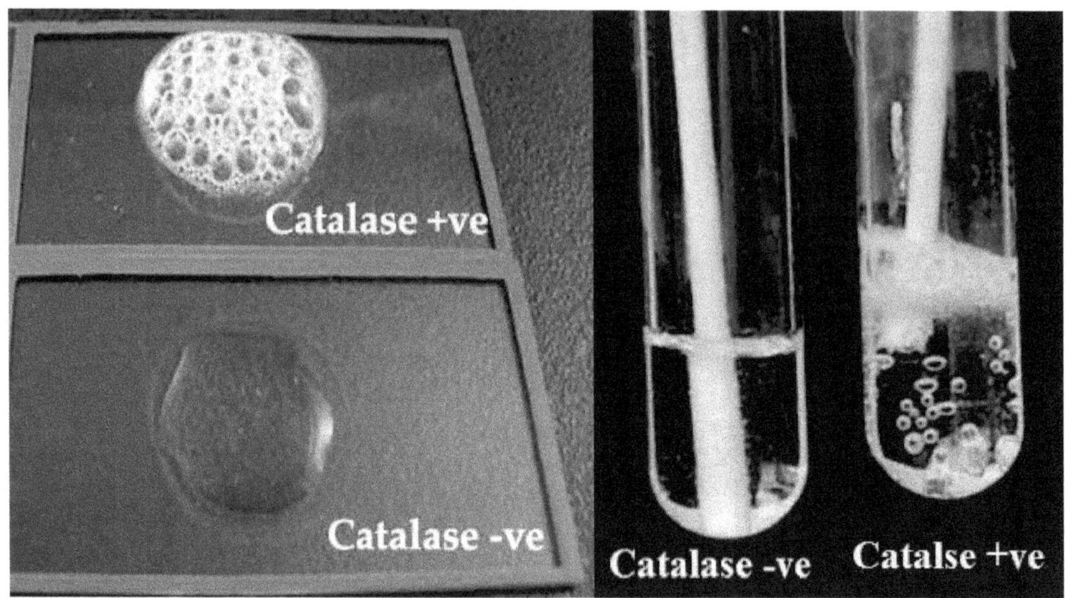

Results of Catalase Test

In the result of the catalase test it has been found to separate between staphylococci which is gram positive from streptococci and enterococci which is gram negative and Bacillus which is catalase-positive from catalase-negative Clostridium spp.

Precautions:

1. The test organisms should not be taken from blood agar culture. Red Blood cells contain catalase and their presence will give a false positive test.

2. Culture should be 18 to 24 hours old.

3. Hydrogen peroxide must be fresh as it is very unstable.

4. Iron wire loop should not be used.

5. Some bacteria produce a peroxidase that catalyzes a breakdown of hydrogen peroxide causing the reaction to be weakly positive; (a few bubbles elaborated slowly). This should not be confused with a truly positive reaction.

6. Do not add organism to reagent, particularly if iron-containing inoculating loops are used. Iron containing loops will cause false positive test results if exposed to hydrogen peroxide.

CHAPTER EIGHTEEN

Objective no – 18: Isolation of Pure Culture of Micro-organism

The common plating techniques employed in microbiology are Streak Plate Method, Spread Plate Method and Pour Plate Method.

1. Streak Plate Method

This method was developed by two bacteriologists, Leoffler and Gaffkey in the laboratory of Robert Koch. This method is routinely employed for the isolation of bacteria in pure culture. In this method a sterilized inoculating loop or transfer needle is dipped into a suitable diluted suspension of microorganisms which is then streaked on the surface of an already solidified agar plate to make a series of parallel, non-overlapping streaks. The process is known as streaking and the plate so prepared is called a streak plate. The main objective of the streak plate method is to produce well separated colonies of bacteria from concentrated suspensions of cells.

A sterilized inoculating needle with a loop made up of either platinum or nichrome wire is used for streaking. One loopful of specimen is transferred onto the surface of the agar plate in a sterile petridish and streaked across the surface in the form of a zig-zag line. This process is repeated thrice to streak out the bacteria on the agar plate so that some individual bacteria are separated from each other. The first streak will contain more organisms than the second and the second more than the third and so on. The last streaks should thin so on. The last streaks should thin out the culture sufficiently to give isolate colonies. The successful isolation depends on spatial separation of single cells. Each colony usually represents the growth from a single organism when such a plate is incubated colonies will appear on the surface of the medium. Because of the high concentration of water in agar, some water of condensation forms in petriplate during incubation. Moisture is likely to drip from the cover to the surface of the agar and spread out, resulting in a confluent mass of growth and running individual colony formation. To avoid this, petriplates are routinely incubated bottom side up. Pure colonies can be obtained from well isolated colonies by transferring a small portion of each to separate culturemedia.

2. Spread Plate Method

The spread plate technique is used for the separation of a dilute, mixed population of the microorganisms so that individual colonies can be isolated. In this technique, a small volume of dilute microbial mixture is transferred to the center of an agar plate and spread evenly over the surface with a sterile L-shaped bent glass rod, while the petridish is spun, at some stage, single cells will be deposited with the bent glass rod on the agar surface. Incubate the agar plate at 37ºC for 24 hours, in the inverted position. The dispersed cells will develop into isolated colonies. Because the number of colonies will be equal to the number of viable organisms in the sample spread plates can be used to count the microbial population.

3. Pour Plate Method

In pour plate method, successive dilutions of the inoculum (serially diluting the original specimen) are added into sterile petriplate to which is poured melted and cooled (42ºC - 45ºC) agar medium and thoroughly mixed by rotating the plates which is then allowed to solidify. After incubation, the plates are examined for the presence of individual colonies. The pure colonies may be isolated and transferred into test tube culture media for making pure cultures. This technique is employed to estimate the viable bacterial count in asuspension.

4. Micromanipulator Method

- In this technique, a microscope is used to pick out a single bacterial cell with the help of a device known as micromanipulator. A single viable cell may be transferred on the culture medium to develop turbidity.
- Enrichment, selective and indicator media are widely used for the isolation of pathogens from specimens such as faeces with varied flora.
- Pure culture may be obtained by pre-treatment of specimens with appropriate bactericidal substances which destroy the unwanted bacteria. This method is the standard practice for the isolation of tubercle bacilli from sputum and other clinical specimen.
- Obligate aerobes and anaerobes may be separated by cultivation under aerobic or anaerobic conditions.
- Microorganisms can also be violated by controlling physical environment especially temperature. Bacteria with different optimum growth temperature can be separated by incubating at different temperature. Only thermophiles bacteria grow to 60°C. A mixture containing vegetative and spore forming bacteria can be separated by heating at 80°C. In this method, the bacteria in the vegetative state will be eliminated. This method is useful for the isolation of tetanus bacilli from dust and similar sources.
- Separation between motile and non-motile bacteria can be effected using Craigie's tube. This consists of a tube of semisolid agar with a narrow tube open at both ends placed in the center of the medium in such a way that it projects above the level of the medium. The mixture is inoculated into the central tube, the motile bacteria alone transverse the agar and appear at the top of the medium outside the central tube.

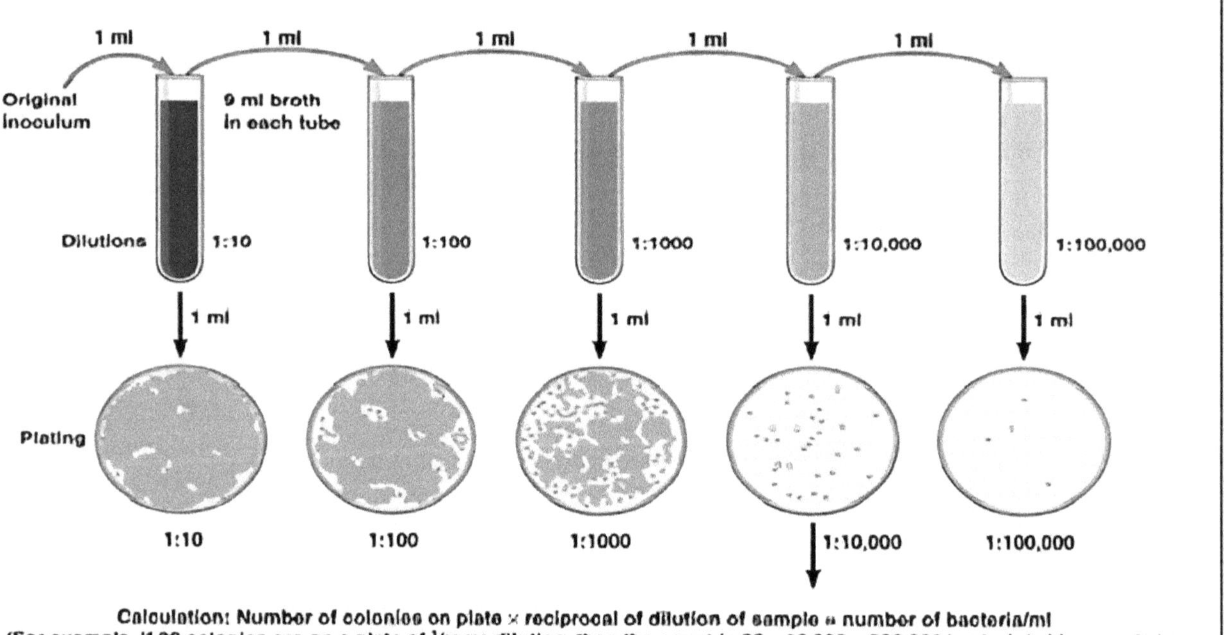

Serial Dilution method to obtain the pure culture

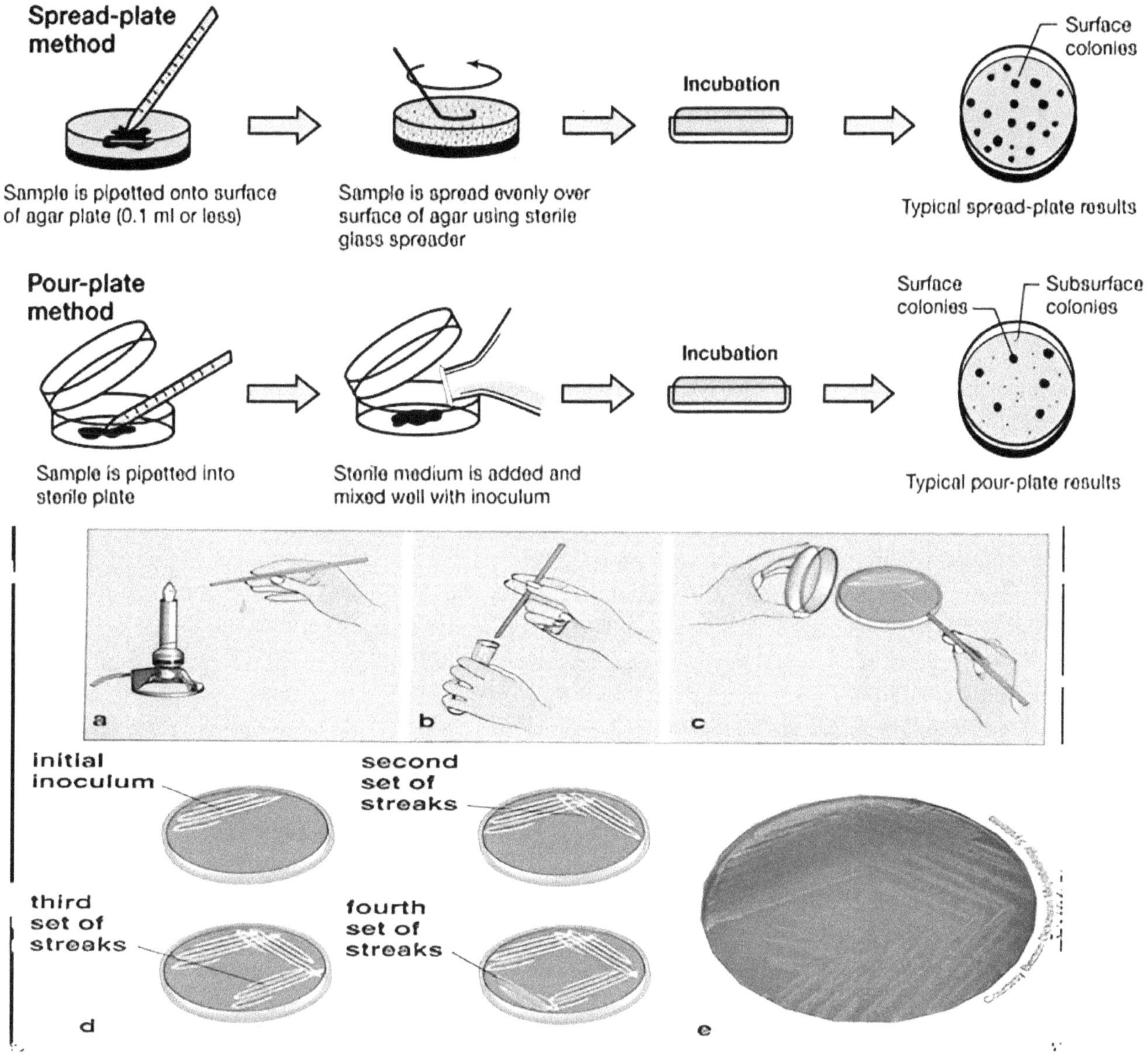

Different plating Techniques for Prepration of Pure Culture

CHAPTER NINETEEN

Objective no- 19: To calculate the total colony forming units of given sample

Microorganism is an organism that is microscopic or submicroscopic, which is too small to be seen under naked eyes. However, the numbers of microorganisms in a given sample are required to know in certain aspect such as dairy industries, diseases investigation, and so on. Because of this, a variety of methods have been developed for the enumeration of microorganisms like direct microscopic counts, filtration and viable plate counts. Among the methods of enumeration, viable plate counts are being used most frequently to measure bacterial populations. In viable plate counts, we are measuring the number of viable cells, unlike the microscopic counts which cannot distinguish live from dead cells. However, it takes some time for the visible colonies to grow. Before doing plate counts, serial dilutions are required. This is because it is hard to count more than 300 colonies on an agar plate if we inoculated directly from the original bacterial suspension or sample without serial dilutions. To complete plate counts, we could either use pour plate method or spread plate method and each of them have their advantages and limitations. All the visible colonies are calculated and represented as colony forming units (CFU). Then, the CFU is multiplied with the corresponding dilution factor. As a result, the population of original sample is known. The objectives of this experiment are to learn the process of enumeration to determine the number of microorganisms in a sample and utilize two methods in enumeration which are pour plate method and spread plate method. Pour Plate Method The pour plate, like other viable plate count methods, involves adding a sample to a solid medium that will support microbial growth incubating the plates so that each bacterial cell multiplies to form a colony, and counting the number of colonies that develop. Generally we have no idea of the number of bacteria in a sample, so it is almost always necessary to prepare a dilution series to ensure that you will obtain a dilution containing a reasonable number of bacteria to count.

Requirements: Tap water or pond water sample Nutrient agar pours (15 mL/tube) Sterile dilution water blanks (99 mL) Sterile Petri plates Pipettes (1 mL, sterile) Pipette bulb or mechanical pump Marking pen Water bath at 50°C

Method:

a. Six nutrient agar pours are melted in a boiling water bath. After they liquefy, they are mixed and placed in a 50°C water bath until they are ready to use.

b. Three 99 mL dilution blanks are labeled as 10-2, 10-4, and 10-6 respectively. Six Petri plates are labeled 10-2 through 10-7 .

c. The unknown sample is shaken to ensure an even distribution of microorganisms (generally shaking side to side for 25 times). 1 mL of sample is removed aseptically with a sterile pipette and transfer it to the 10-2 dilution blank.

d. The dilution blank is shaken vigorously to distribute the bacteria evenly.

e. Using a new sterile pipette, 0.1 mL and 1.0 mL are transferred aseptically from the 10-2 dilution to the agar plates labeled 10-3 (0.1 mL)and 10-2 (1 mL)respectively. With the same pipette, an additional 1.0 mL is removed from the 10-2 dilution blank and transferred to the 10-4 dilution blank. The original 1 mL of sample has now been diluted 1 part in a total of 10,000 parts.

f. The shaking procedure is repeated for the 10-4 blank and 0.1 mL and 1.0 mL portions are transferred from this dilution bottle with a new pipette to the plates labeled 10-5 (0.1 mL)and 10-4 (l mL).

g. This same procedure is repeated to form a 10-6 dilution blank from which you will establish 10-7 (0.1 mL)and 10-6 (1.0 mL) plates.

h. A tube of melted agar (50°C)is poured aseptically into each Petri plate to which already added a dilution of the sample. The plate is swirled to mix the sample with the agar. The agar is made sure does not run over the edges of the plate. The lid is replaced. The agar is allowed to cool and solidity.

a. The inverted plates are incubated at 30°C.

j. After incubation, the colonies are counted on each plate. Both the colonies on the agar surface and the colonies growing within the agar must be counted. The colonies are counted by marking their position on the back of the Petri plates with a marking pen. This aid in keeping track of those colonies previously counted and avoids recounts. Counts are recorded. If a plate has more than 300 colonies record it as TNTC (too numerous to count).

k. From the plate-count data, the concentration of bacteria in the original sample is calculated. For statistical reasons only plates with between 30 and 300 colonies are used in this calculation. Each colony forming unit (CFU) represents the progeny of a single cell. Therefore, the number of bacterial cells in the original sample is determined by multiplying the number of colonies on a dilution plate by the corresponding dilution factor. For example, if you counted 200 colonies on the 10-4 plate, 200 x 10,000 = 2,000,000 colonies or 2 x 106 viable cells/mL were present in the original sample. Generally replicates of each dilution are plated, and the mean count recorded.

CHAPTER TWENTY

Objective no – 20: To Characterize and identify the micro-organisms on the basis of specific morphological and biochemical characteristics

1. Escherichia coli

- Section : Facultative, Gram negative rods
- Family : Enterobacteriaceace
- Genus : *Escherichia*
- Species : *coli*

  - Common coliform bacterium used in laboratory practices
  - The bacterium is rod shaped generally 1.3 x 2.5 μm in size
  - Gram negative, facultatively anaerobe, motile having peritrichous flagella
  - It causes diarrhea due to the presence of enterotoxins.
  - It is catalase positive and oxidase negative

Colony Characteristics
a. On Nutrient Agar
Small, regular, circular, translucent colonies
b. On Mac conkey Agar
Small, regular, circular, lactose fermenting colonies
Biochemical Tests:

Biochemical tests of *E.coli*		
1	Sugar Fermentation Tests	
a	Glucose	Fermented with acid & gas production
b	Lactose	Fermented with acid & gas production
c	Sucrose	Fermented with acid & gas production
2	Oxidation – Fermentation test	Fermentati ve
3	Mannitol Motility Test	Motile with diffused growth
4	Indole Production	–
5	Methyl Red	–
6	Voges – Proskauer	·
7	Citrate Utilization	·
8	Nitrate Reduction	–
9	Urease test	·
10	Triple Sugar Iron Agar	A/A with gas production & no H_2S production

Biochemical Tests for *E. Coli*

2. Klebsiella

- Section : Facultative, Gram negative rods
- Family : Enterobacteriaceace
- Genus : *Klebsiella*

- No specific growth requirements and grow well on standard laboratory media
- Grows best between 35 and 37°C and at pH 7.2
- The bacterium is rod shaped, non-motile
- Gram negative, facultatively anaerobe
- It is catalase positive and oxidase negative

Colony Characteristics
a. On Nutrient Agar
Large, regular, convex, opaque, mucoid colonies
b. On Mac conkey Agar
Large, regular, convex, opaque, mucoid, lactose fermenting colonies
Biochemical Tests:

Biochemical tests of *Klebsiella*		
1	Sugar Fermentation Tests	
a	Glucose	Fermented with acid & gas production
b	Lactose	Fermented with acid & gas production
c	Sucrose	Fermented with acid & gas production
2	Oxidation – Fermentation test	Fermentative with gas production
3	Mannitol Motility Test	Motile , growth only on stab line
4	Indole Production	.
5	Methyl Red	.
6	Voges – Proskauer	–
7	Citrate Utilization	–
8	Nitrate Reduction	–
9	Urease test	–
10	Triple Sugar Iron Agar	A/A with gas production & no H_2S production

Biochemical Tests for *Klebsiella*

3. *Pseudomonas*

- Section : Facultative, gram negative rods
- Family : Enterobacteriaceace
- Genus : *Pseudomonas*

  - The cells are straight or slightly curved of 1.5 – 5.0 x 0.5-1.0 µ m in size
  - Aerobic and motile
  - Some species are pathogenic to human, animals and plants
  - They are catalase and oxidase positive

Colony Characteristics
a. On Nutrient Agar
Medium, regular, flat, translucent colonies with greenish pigmentation
b. On Mac conkey Agar
Small, irregular, flat, translucent, non-lactose fermenting colonies
Biochemical Tests:

Biochemical tests of *Pseudomonas*		
1	Sugar Fermentation Tests	
a	Glucose	Fermented with acid & no gas production
b	Lactose	Non-fermentative
c	Sucrose	Non-fermentative
2	Oxidation – Fermentation test	Oxidative
3	Mannitol Motility Test	Fermented with diffused growth
4	Indole Production	-
5	Methyl Red	-
6	Voges – Proskauer	-
7	Citrate Utilization	–
8	Nitrate Reduction	–
9	Urease test	-
10	Triple Sugar Iron Agar	K/K with gas production & H_2S production

Biochemical Tests for *Pseudomonas*

4. *Staphylococcus aureus*

- Section : Facultative, gram positive cocci
- Family : Staphylococcaceae
- Genus : *Staphylococcus*
- Species : *aureus*

  - They appear round (cocci) and form in grape-like clusters.
  - Non-Motile
  - It is a common cause of skin infections, respiratory disease and food poisoning.
  - It is catalase and coagulase positive

Colony Characteristics
a. On Nutrient Agar
Small, regular, circular, entire, smooth, convex, opaque, golden yellow colonies
b. On Mac conkey Agar
Small, regular, circular, entire, smooth, convex, opaque, lactose fermenting colonies
Biochemical Tests:

		Biochemical tests of *S. aureus*	
1	Sugar Fermentation Tests		
a	Glucose		Fermented with acid only
b	Lactose		Fermented with acid only
c	Sucrose		Fermented with acid only
2	Oxidation – Fermentation test		Fermentative
3	Mannitol Motility Test		Fermentative and non - motile
4	Indole Production		-
5	Methyl Red		–
6	Voges – Proskauer		–
7	Citrate Utilization		-
8	Nitrate Reduction		–
9	Urease test		–
10	Triple Sugar Iron Agar		A/A without gas production & H_2S production

Biochemical Tests for *S. aureus*

Important Media Composition

Types of culture media based on consistency/ physical state

1. Solid Media

a. Nutrient agar

Peptone 5.0

Sodium chloride 5.0

Peptone 1.5

Yeast extract 1.5

Agar 15.0

Final pH (at 25°C) 7.4±0.2

b. MacConkey agar

Pancreatic Digest of Gelatin 17.0

Peptone from Meat 1.5

Peptone from Casein 1.5

Lactose 10.0

Sodium Chloride 5.0

Bile Salts 1.5

Agar 15.0*

Neutral Red 0.03

Crystal Violet 0.001

Final pH 7.1 ± 0.2 at 25°C

c. Blood agar

Peptone 10.0

Tryptose 10.0

Sodium chloride 5.0

Agar 15.0

Final pH at 25°C: 7.3 ±0.2

d. Chocolate agar

Casein/Animal Tissue Digest 15.0g

Cornstarch 1.0g

Sodium chloride 5.0g

Dipotassium Phosphate 4.0g

Monopotassium Phosphate 1.0g

Hemoglobin solution 2%

Coenzyme enrichment 10.0ml

Agar 10.0g

Final pH 7.2 ± 0.2 (at 25°C)

2. Semi-solid media

a. Stuart's and Amies media

Sodium glycerophosphate 10.00 gm/lit.

Sodium thioglycollate 1.00 gm/lit.

CaCl2.2H2O 0.10 gm/lit.

Methylene Blue 0.002 gm/lit.

pH at 25 °C :7.4 ± 0.2

b. Hugh and Leifson's oxidation fermentation medium

Peptone (tryptone) 2.0 g

Sodium chloride 5.0 g

Glucose (or other carbohydrate) 10.0 g

Bromthymol blue 0.03 g

Agar 3.0 g

Dipotassium phosphate 0.30 g

pH at 25 °C : 7.1

c. Mannitol motility media

Mannitol 2.0 g/L

Potassium nitrate 1.0 g/L.

1% Phenol red solution 4 ml/L.

pH at 25 °C : 7.6.

3. Liquid media

a. Nutrient broth

Peptone 5.0

Sodium chloride 5.0

Peptone 1.5

Yeast extract 1.5

Final pH (at 25°C) 7.4±0.2

b. Tryptic soy broth

Casein peptone (pancreatic) 17 g/L

Dipotassium hydrogen phosphate, 2.5 g/L

Glucose 2.5 g/L

Sodium chloride 5 g/L

Soya peptone (papain digest.) 3 g/L

Final pH (at 25°C) 7.4±0.2

c. MR-VP broth

Buffered peptone 7.0 g/L

Dextrose 5.0 g/L

Dipotassium phosphate 5.0 g/L

Final

pH (at 25°C) 6.9±0.2

d. Phenol red carbohydrate broth

Trypticase or proteone peptone No. 10 g

NaCl 5 g

Beef extract (optional) 1 g

Phenol red 0.018 g

(7.2 ml of 0.25% phenol red solution)

Sucrose 10 g

pH (at 25°C) 7.4 ± 0.2.

List of Culture media used in Microbiology with their intended uses

Alkaline peptone water

Alkaline peptone water is an enrichment broth used for the isolation of small numbers of Vibrio and Aeromonas organisms from stool specimens.

Anaerobic blood agar (CDC)

The Centers for Disease Control and Prevention (CDC) formulation of anaerobic blood agar is a general-purpose medium used for the isolation and cultivation of anaerobic bacteria.

Ashdown agar

Ashdown agar is a selective and differential medium for the isolation of Pseudomonas pseudomallei.

Bacillus cereus medium

B. cereus medium is an enriched medium used for the isolation of B. cereus.

Bismuth sulfite agar

Bismuth sulfite agar is a highly selective and differential medium used for the isolation of Salmonella enterica serovar Typhi and other enteric bacilli.

Blood agar

It is the same as Columbia agar with 5% sheep blood.

Blood culture media

All blood culture medium formulations are based on a nutrient peptone broth with variations due to hydrolysis or digestion of the source protein.

Bordet-Gengou medium

Bordet-Gengou medium is an enriched medium used for the isolation and cultivation of Bordetella pertussis from clinical specimens.

Brain heart infusion agar

Brain heart infusion agar is a general-purpose medium used for the isolation of a wide variety of pathogens, including yeasts, molds, and bacteria.

Brain heart infusion agar with 7% horse blood and brain heart infusion agar with 1% serum

Brain heart infusion agar with horse blood or serum enriches the medium for isolation of Helicobacter spp.

Brain heart infusion broth

Brain heart infusion broth is a general-purpose clear liquid medium that is used to cultivate a wide variety of organisms. Formulations with 6.5% NaCl are used for the isolation of salt-tolerant streptococci, formulations with 0.1% agar that reduce O2 tension favor anaerobes, and formulations with Fildes enrichment are used for the isolation of fastidious organisms such as Haemophilus and Neisseria.

Brain heart infusion-vancomycin agar

Brain heart infusion-vancomycin agar is a selective medium used for the isolation of vancomycin-resistant enterococci. The base is brain heart infusion agar. Vancomycin (6g/ml) is added to select for vancomycin-resistant enterococci.

Brucella agar

Brucella agar is a medium designed originally for the purpose of isolating Brucella spp. from dairy products.

Brucella Broth

Brucella Broth is a liquid medium that is used to cultivate Campylobacter species and to identify the organisms to the species level.

Buffered glycerol saline

Buffered glycerol saline is a multipurpose transport medium. The transport medium has been used for the isolation of bacteria, such as Aeromonas spp., as well as viruses. In addition, glycerol-containing media may also be used for long-term storage of isolates and for transport and storage of biopsy specimens.

Charcoal selective medium

Charcoal selective medium is an enriched selective medium used for the isolation of Campylobacter species.

Chocolate agar

Chocolate agar is a general-purpose medium used for the isolation and detection of a wide variety of microorganisms, including fastidious species such as Neisseria and Haemophilus.

DNA-toluidine blue agar

DNA-toluidine blue agar is a differential medium used most commonly for the detection and differentiation of Staphylococcus spp.

Egg yolk agar (modified McClung-Toabe agar)

Egg yolk agar medium (modified McClung-Toabe agar) is a selective and differential medium used for the isolation and differentiation of Clostridium spp.

Eosin-methylene blue (EMB) agar

EMB agar is a selective and differential medium used for the isolation and differentiation of enteric pathogens from contaminated clinical specimens.

Fastidious anaerobic agar (Fusobacterium selective agar)

Fastidious anaerobic agar is an enriched sheep blood medium used for the isolation and cultivation of anaerobic organisms.

Heart infusion agar and broth

Heart infusion agar and broth are general-purpose media used for the isolation of a variety of microorganisms. Incorporation with 5% rabbit blood allows detection of the more fastidious Actinomyces.

Lowenstein-Jensen medium

Lowenstein-Jensen medium is an enriched nonselective medium used for the isolation and cultivation of mycobacteria. It is similar to the American Trudeau Society medium in its content and its ability to grow mycobacteria.

MacConkey agar

MacConkey agar is a selective and differential medium used for the isolation of gram-negative organisms. The nutritive base includes a variety of peptones. The medium is made selective by the incorporation of bile (although at levels less than those used in other enteric media) and crystal violet, which inhibit gram-positive organisms, especially enterococci and staphylococci.

MacConkey agar with sorbitol (SMAC)

SMAC is a selective and differential medium used for the isolation and differentiation of sorbitol-negative E. coli.

MacConkey broth

MacConkey broth is a differential medium containing the indicator bromcresol purple used for the detection of coliform organisms from contaminated food, water, or stools.

Mannitol salt agar

Mannitol salt agar is a selective and differential medium used for the isolation of S. aureus.

Martin-Lewis agar

Martin-Lewis agar is an enriched and selective medium for the isolation of N. gonorrhoeae.

Mueller-Hinton agar with 2% NaCl

Mueller-Hinton agar with 2% NaCl is a selective medium used for testing the susceptibility of Staphylococcus to the penicillinase-resistant penicillins methicillin, nafcillin, and oxacillin by agar dilution or with the gradient-based system (E test).

Mueller-Hinton broth

Mueller-Hinton broth is a magnesium and calcium cation adjusted liquid medium used in procedures for susceptibility testing of aerobic gram-positive and gram-negative organisms by both macro dilution and microdilution methods.

NAG medium

NAG medium is an enriched and selective medium used for the isolation and cultivation of Haemophilus species from clinical specimens with mixed flora.

Neomycin-vancomycin agar

Neomycin-vancomycin agar is an enriched and selective medium that is particularly good for the isolation and cultivation of Fusobacterium from clinical specimens.

Peptone yeast extract broth

Peptone yeast extract broth is used in the analysis of metabolic products by gas-liquid chromatography because there is negligible acid volatility within the medium.

Salmonella-shigella agar

Salmonella-shigella agar is a selective and differential medium used for the isolation and differentiation of

Streptococcus selective agar

Streptococcus selective agar is a selective medium for the detection of streptococci. The agar base is Columbia agar.

Sucrose-phosphate-glutamate transport medium

Sucrose-phosphate-glutamate transport medium is used for the maintenance and transport of Chlamydia species and viruses.

Thiosulfate citrate bile salt sucrose (TCBS)

TCBS is a highly selective and differential medium for the recovery of Vibrio spp. except for Vibrio hollisae and Vibrio cincinnatiensis.

Tryptic or Trypticase soy agar base with 5% sheep blood

Tryptic or Trypticase soy agar base with 5% sheep blood is a general-purpose medium used for the isolation of a wide variety of organisms. The use of sheep blood provides an excellent means of interpretation of hemolytic reactions, especially those of Streptococcus spp.

Tryptic or Trypticase soy broth

Tryptic or Trypticase soy broth is a general-purpose clear liquid medium used for the cultivation of a wide variety of organisms. It is also recommended by the CLSI for the preparation of inoculum for Kirby-Bauer disk diffusion susceptibility testing and is the CLSI's choice as a sterility testing medium. Formulations with 6.5% NaCl exist for the purposes of differentiating enterococcal species or salt-tolerant streptococci. Fildes enrichment is added to cultivate fastidious organisms such as Haemophilus spp.

Xylose-lysine-desoxycholate (XLD) agar

Xylose-lysine-desoxycholate agar is a selective and differential medium used for the isolation and differentiation of enteric pathogens from clinical specimens. This medium is more supportive of fastidious enteric organisms such as Shigella. For Salmonella, which contains the lysine enzyme, this reaction reverts the pH to an alkaline state and the colony appears to be transparent or red with a black center. A number of other similar media for isolation of enteric pathogens exist, including xylose-galactosidase medium, which is more specific for Aeromonas spp.

Yersinia selective agar

It is similar to Cefsulodin-Irgasan-novobiocin medium.

Bibliography

1. HPA (UK) BSOP 54: Standard Operating Procedure for the Inoculation of Culture Media, issued by Standards Unit, Evaluations and Standards Laboratory, HPA (UK).

2. McClelland, R., 2001. Gram's stain the key to microbiology. Medical Laboratory Observer, Available from: http://www.mlo-online.com/ce/pdfs/apr01.pdf.

3. Jorgensen., et al. Manual of Clinical Microbiology, American Society for Microbiology, Washington, D.C.

4. MacFaddin, J.F., 1985. Media for Isolation, Cultivation, Identification, Maintenance of Bacteria, Vol. I. Williams & Wilkins, Baltimore, MD.

5. Collee J. G., Fraser A. G., Marimon B. P., Simmons A., (Eds.), 1996. Mackie and McCartney Practical Medical Microbiology, 14th Ed., Churchill Livingstone.

6. Finegold S. M. and Baron E. J., (Ed.), 1986. Bailey and Scott's Diagnostic Microbiology, 7th Edition, The C.V. Mosby Company, St. Louis.

7. MacWilliams, M., 2013. Indole Test Protocol. American Society for Microbiology Peer-reviewed.

8. Crookshank, E. M., 1886. An introduction to practical bacteriology. J. H. Vail and Co., New York, NY.

10. Isenberg, H.D., Clinical Microbiology Procedures Handbook, Vol. I, II & III. American Society for Microbiology, Washington, D.C.

11. Voges, O. and Proskauer, B., 1898. Zeit. Hyg.; 28:20-32.

12. Harley, J. P., 2005. Laboratory exercises in microbiology, 6th ed. McGraw Hill, New York, NY.

13. Reddy, C. A., (ed.). 2007. Methods for general and molecular microbiology, 3rd ed. ASM Press, Washington, DC.

14. Davis, B. D., Dulbecco, R., Eisen, H.N. and Ginsberg, H.S., 1980. Microbiology, 3rd ed. Harper and Row Publishers, Hagerstown, MD.

15. Alexander, S. K. and Strete, D., 2001. Microbiology: a photographic atlas for the laboratory. Benjamin Cummings, San Francisco, CA.

16. Nobre, G. N., Charrua, M. J., and Silva, M.M., 1987. The oxidase test in yeasts of medical importance. J. Med. Microbiol. 23: 359-361.

17. Joan Petersen & Susan McLaughlin Associate Professors (Biological Sciences and Geology) at Queensborough Community College.

18. Aebi, H., 1984. Catalase in vitro. Methods Enzymol. 105: 121-126.

19. Ausubel, F. M., Brent R., Kingston, R.E., Moore, D.D., Seidman, J.G., Smith, J. A., and Struhl, K., 1987. Current protocols in molecular biology. John Wiley & Sons, Inc., New York.

20. Bauer AW (1966) Antibiotic susceptibility testing by a standardized single disc method. American Journal of Clinical Pathology, 45: 149-158.

21. Sharma, P.D. Microbiology and Plant Pathology.

22. Sharma, O.P. Diversity of Microbes and Cryptogams, Mc Graw Hill Publication.

23. Hengen P. N., 1994. Methods and Reagents: Disposal of Ethidium Bromide, Trends in Biochemical Sciences 19 (6): 257-258. doi:10.1016/0968-0004(94)90152-X.

24. Joanne Willcy and Linda Sherwood and Christopher J. Woolverton "Prescott's Microbiology" Mc Graw Hill 2017, 10th edition.

25.https://www.academia.edu/19589769/Colony_Forming_Unit_Calculations_Using_Spread_Plate_Method.

26. https://reach.cdc.gov/jobaid/how-perform-oxidase-test.

27. https://nios.ac.in/media/documents/dmlt/Microbiology/Lesson-06.pdf.

28.https://knowledge.carolina.com/discipline/life-science/microbiology/12-safe-practices-for-the-microbiology-laboratory/

29. https://www.sigmaaldrich.com/IN/en/applications/microbiological-testing/microbial-culture-media-preparation?srsltid=AfmBOooleZW4QIPPW6rp3qC3HE7rIwL2m7V_KiL9Ll3-CsCNZCZvela9.

30.https://www.cdc.gov/labtraining/docs/job_aids/biochemicals_gram_positive_organism_id/Colonial_Characteristics_Branded_508.pdf.

31. https://www.ncbi.nlm.nih.gov/pmc/articles/PMC10178692/

32. http://www.biolab.rs/wp-content/uploads/2018/01/Chocolate-Agar.pdf.

33. https://patents.google.com/patent/DE4216078C1/en.

34. https://www.tmmedia.in/wp-content/uploads/TD/TD-TM-672.pdf.

35. https://www.cdc.gov/training/quicklearns/biosafety/